MznLnx

Missing Links Exam Preps

Exam Prep for

Advanced Financial Accounting

Baker, Lembke, King, 6th Edition

The MznLnx Exam Prep is your link from the texbook and lecture to your exams.
The MznLnx Exam Preps are unauthorized and comprehensive reviews of your textbooks.

All material provided by MznLnx and Rico Publications (c) 2010
Textbook publishers and textbook authors do not particpate in or contribute to these reviews.

MznLnx

Rico
Publications

Exam Prep for Advanced Financial Accounting
6th Edition
Baker, Lembke, King

Publisher: Raymond Houge
Assistant Editor: Michael Rouger
Text and Cover Designer: Lisa Buckner
Marketing Manager: Sara Swagger
Project Manager, Editorial Production: Jerry Emerson
Art Director: Vernon Lowerui

Product Manager: Dave Mason
Editorial Assitant: Rachel Guzmanji
Pedagogy: Debra Long
Cover Image: Jim Reed/Getty Images
Text and Cover Printer: City Printing, Inc.
Compositor: Media Mix, Inc.

(c) 2010 Rico Publications
ALL RIGHTS RESERVED. No part of this work covered by the copyright may be reproduced or used in any form or by an means--graphic, electronic, or mechanical, including photocopying, recording, taping, Web distribution, information storage, and retrieval systems, or in any other manner--without the written permission of the publisher.

Printed in the United States
ISBN:

For more information about our products, contact us at:
Dave.Mason@RicoPublications.com

For permission to use material from this text or product, submit a request online to:
Dave.Mason@RicoPublications.com

Contents

CHAPTER 1
Intercorporate Acquisitions and Investments in Other Entities — 1

CHAPTER 2
Reporting Intercorporate Interests — 8

CHAPTER 3
The Reporting Entity and Consolidated Financial Statements — 15

CHAPTER 4
Consolidation as of the Date of Acquisition — 21

CHAPTER 5
Consolidation Following Acquisition — 26

CHAPTER 6
Intercorporate Transfers: Noncurrent Assets — 30

CHAPTER 7
Intercompany Inventory Transactions — 33

CHAPTER 8
Intercompany Indebtedness — 36

CHAPTER 9
Consolidation Ownership Issues — 38

CHAPTER 10
Additional Consolidation Reporting Issues — 42

CHAPTER 11
Multinational Accounting — 47

CHAPTER 12
Multinational Accounting: Translation of Foreign Entity Statements — 58

CHAPTER 13
Segment and Interim Reporting — 64

CHAPTER 14
SEC Reporting — 69

CHAPTER 15
Partnerships: Formation, Operation, and Changes in Membership — 79

CHAPTER 16
Partnerships: Liquidation — 85

CHAPTER 17
Governmental Entities: Introduction and General Fund Accounting — 87

CHAPTER 18
Governmental Entities: Special Funds and Government-wide Financial Statements — 96

CHAPTER 19
Not-for-Profit Entities — 103

CHAPTER 20
Corporations in Financial Difficulty — 108

ANSWER KEY — 112

TO THE STUDENT

COMPREHENSIVE

The *MznLnx* Exam Prep series is designed to help you pass your exams. Editors at MznLnx review your textbooks and then prepare these practice exams to help you master the textbook material. Unlike study guides, workbooks, and practice tests provided by the texbook publisher and textbook authors, *MznLnx* gives you **all** of the material in each chapter in exam form, not just samples, so you can be sure to nail your exam.

MECHANICAL

The MznLnx Exam Prep series creates exams that will help you learn the subject matter as well as test you on your understanding. Each question is designed to help you master the concept. Just working through the exams, you gain an understanding of the subject--its a simple mechanical process that produces success.

INTEGRATED STUDY GUIDE AND REVIEW

MznLnx is not just a set of exams designed to test you, its also a comprehensive review of the subject content. Each exam question is also a review of the concept, making sure that you will get the answer correct without having to go to other sources of material. You learn as you go! Its the easiest way to pass an exam.

HUMOR

Studying can be tedious and dry. MznLnx's instructional design includes moderate humor within the exam questions on occassion, to break the tedium and revitalize the brain

Chapter 1. Intercorporate Acquisitions and Investments in Other Entities　　　　1

1. _____ is a form of corporation equity ownership represented in the securities. It is a stock whose dividends are based on market fluctuations. It is dangerous in comparison to preferred shares and some other investment options, in that in the event of bankruptcy, _____ investors receive their funds after preferred stock holders, bondholders, creditors, etc. On the other hand, common shares on average perform better than preferred shares or bonds over time.

   a. Stock split
   b. Common stock
   c. 3M Company
   d. Growth investing

2. _____ are financial statements that factor the holding company's subsidiaries into its aggregated accounting figure. It is a representation of how the holding company is doing as a group. The consolidated accounts should provide a true and fair view of the financial and operating conditions of the group.

   a. Redemption value
   b. Replacement cost
   c. Committee on Accounting Procedure
   d. Consolidated financial statements

3. An _____ is a mostly hierarchical concept of subordination of entities that collaborate and contribute to serve one common aim.

Organizations are a variant of clustered entities. The structure of an organization is usually set up in many a styles, dependent on their objectives and ambience.

   a. ABC Television Network
   b. AMEX
   c. AIG
   d. Organizational structure

4. A _____ is a company that owns enough voting stock in another firm to control management and operations by influencing or electing its board of directors; the second company being deemed as a subsidiary of the _____. The definition of a _____ differs from jurisdiction to jurisdiction, with the definition normally being defined by way of laws dealing with companies in that jurisdiction.

The _____-subsidiary company relationship is defined by Part 1.2, Division 6, Section 46 of the Corporations Act 2001 (Cth), which states:

A body corporate (in this section called the first body) is a subsidiary of another body corporate if, and only if:

   (a) the other body:

   (i) controls the composition of the first body's board; or

   (ii) is in a position to cast, or control the casting of, more than one-half of the maximum number of votes that might be cast at a general meeting of the first body; or

   (iii) holds more than one-half of the issued share capital of the first body (excluding any part of that issued share capital that carries no right to participate beyond a specified amount in a distribution of either profits or capital); or

   (b) the first body is a subsidiary of a subsidiary of the other body.

a. BMC Software, Inc. b. Parent company
c. 3M Company d. Subsidiary

5. A _____, in business matters, is an entity that is controlled by a bigger and more powerful entity. The controlled entity is called a company, corporation, or limited liability company, and the controlling entity is called its parent (or the parent company.) The reason for this distinction is that a lone company cannot be a _____ of any organization; only an entity representing a legal fiction as a separate entity can be a _____.

a. Subsidiary b. Parent company
c. BMC Software, Inc. d. 3M Company

6. _____ are formal records of a business' financial activities.

In British English, including United Kingdom company law, _____ are often referred to as accounts, although the term _____ is also used, particularly by accountants.

_____ provide an overview of a business' financial condition in both short and long term.

a. Statement of retained earnings b. 3M Company
c. Notes to the financial statements d. Financial statements

7. The _____ is a private, not-for-profit organization whose primary purpose is to develop generally accepted accounting principles (GAAP) within the United States in the public's interest. The Securities and Exchange Commission (SEC) designated the _____ as the organization responsible for setting accounting standards for public companies in the U.S. It was created in 1973, replacing the Accounting Principles Board and the Committee on Accounting Procedure of the American Institute of Certified Public Accountants. The _____'s mission is 'to establish and improve standards of financial accounting and reporting for the guidance and education of the public, including issuers, auditors, and users of financial information.'

The _____ is not a governmental body.

a. Financial Accounting Standards Board b. Governmental Accounting Standards Board
c. Public company d. Fannie Mae

8. A _____ is a new organization or entity formed by a split from a larger one, such as a television series based on a pre-existing one, or a new company formed from a university research group or business incubator. In literature, especially in milieu-based popular fictional book series like mysteries, westerns, fantasy or science fiction, the term sub-series is generally used instead of _____, but with essentially the same meaning.

_____s as a descriptive term can also include a dissenting faction of a membership organization, a sect of a cult, or a denomination of a church.

a. Spin-off b. BNSF Railway
c. 3M Company d. BMC Software, Inc.

Chapter 1. Intercorporate Acquisitions and Investments in Other Entities

9. The American Oil Company founded in Baltimore in 1910 and incorporated in 1922 by Louis Blaustein and his son Jacob, but is now part of BP. The firm's innovations included two essential parts of the modern industry- the gasoline tanker truck and the drive-through filling station.

In 1923 the Blausteins sold a half interest in _____ to the Pan American Petroleum ' Transport company in exchange for a guaranteed supply of oil.

a. Information Systems Audit and Control Association
b. International Accounting Standards Committee
c. International Federation of Accountants
d. Amoco

10. A _____ is 'that right which a person has in a contract made with another' (third) person. The typical example is 'if A makes a contract with B that he will pay C a certain sum of money, B has the legal interest in the contract, and C the _____.'

More generally, a _____ is any 'interest of value, worth, or use in property one does not own,' for example, 'the interest that a beneficiary of a trust has in the trust.' More specifically, it could be:

- 'A property interest that inures solely to the benefit of the owner,' or
- Property that 'remains of an estate after the payment of debts and the expenses of administration', or
- The right of a person having a power of appointment to appoint himself.'

Black's Law Dictionary defines _____ as 'Profit, benefit or advantage resulting from a contract, or the ownership of an estate as distinct from the legal ownership or control.' Examples of _____s in mining claims include unrecorded deeds and agreements to share profits, but not mortages and other liens. A _____ is also 'distinguished from the rights of someone like a trustee or official who has responsibility to perform and/or title to the assets but does not share in the benefits.'

a. Beneficial interest
b. Nonacquiescence
c. Headnote
d. Tangible

11. In business or economics a _____ is a combination of two companies into one larger company. Such actions are commonly voluntary and involve stock swap or cash payment to the target. Stock swap is often used as it allows the shareholders of the two companies to share the risk involved in the deal. A _____ can resemble a takeover but result in a new company name (often combining the names of the original companies) and in new branding; in some cases, terming the combination a '_____' rather than an acquisition is done purely for political or marketing reasons.

a. BNSF Railway
b. 3M Company
c. BMC Software, Inc.
d. Merger

12. _____ is a fee paid on borrowed assets. It is the price paid for the use of borrowed money , or, money earned by deposited funds .Assets that are sometimes lent with _____ include money, shares, consumer goods through hire purchase, major assets such as aircraft, and even entire factories in finance lease arrangements. The _____ is calculated upon the value of the assets in the same manner as upon money.

a. ABC Television Network
b. AIG
c. Insolvency
d. Interest

13. _____ is the state or fact of exclusive rights and control over property, which may be an object, land/real estate or intellectual property. An _____ right is also referred to as title.

_____ is the key building block in the development of the capitalist socio-economic system.

   a. ABC Television Network
   b. Encumbrance
   c. Administrative proceeding
   d. Ownership

14. In law, _____ refers to the process by which a company (or part of a company) is brought to an end, and the assets and property of the company redistributed. _____ can also be referred to as winding-up or dissolution, although dissolution technically refers to the last stage of _____. The process of _____ also arises when customs, an authority or agency in a country responsible for collecting and safeguarding customs duties, determines the final computation or ascertainment of the duties or drawback accruing on an entry.
   a. 3M Company
   b. BMC Software, Inc.
   c. Liquidation
   d. Bankruptcy protection

15. An _____ is the buying of one company by another. An _____ may be friendly or hostile. In the former case, the companies cooperate in negotiations; in the latter case, the takeover target is unwilling to be bought or the target's board has no prior knowledge of the offer. _____ usually refers to a purchase of a smaller firm by a larger one. Sometimes, however, a smaller firm will acquire management control of a larger or longer established company and keep its name for the combined entity. This is known as a reverse takeover.
   a. AIG
   b. AMEX
   c. ABC Television Network
   d. Acquisition

16. In business and accounting, _____ are everything of value that is owned by a person or company. It is a claim on the property your income of a borrower. The balance sheet of a firm records the monetary value of the _____ owned by the firm.
   a. Accrual basis accounting
   b. Assets
   c. Accounts receivable
   d. Earnings before interest, taxes, depreciation and amortization

17. In finance, _____ is the process of estimating the potential market value of a financial asset or liability. They can be done on assets (for example, investments in marketable securities such as stocks, options, business enterprises, or intangible assets such as patents and trademarks) or on liabilities (e.g., Bonds issued by a company.) A _____ is required in many contexts including investment analysis, capital budgeting, merger and acquisition transactions, financial reporting, taxable events to determine the proper tax liability, and in litigation.
   a. Daybook
   b. Disclosure
   c. Vyborg Appeal
   d. Valuation

18. _____ in business is an accounting concept that refers to ownership of a company (subsidiary) that is less than 50% of outstanding shares. _____ belongs to other investors and is reported on the consolidated balance sheet of the owning company to reflect the claim on assets belonging to other, non-controlling shareholders. Also, _____ is reported on the consolidated income statement as a share of profit belonging to minority shareholders.
   a. Subledger
   b. Credit memo
   c. Bankruptcy prediction
   d. Minority interest

Chapter 1. Intercorporate Acquisitions and Investments in Other Entities

19. _____ is a specific term used in companies' financial reporting from the company-whole point of view. Because that use excludes the effects of changing ownership interest, an economic measure of _____ is necessary for financial analysis from the shareholders' point of view

_____ is defined by the Financial Accounting Standards Board, or FASB, as 'the change in equity [net assets] of a business enterprise during a period from transactions and other events and circumstances from nonowner sources. It includes all changes in equity during a period except those resulting from investments by owners and distributions to owners.'

_____ is the sum of net income and other items that must bypass the income statement because they have not been realized, including items like an unrealized holding gain or loss from available for sale securities and foreign currency translation gains or losses.

a. BMC Software, Inc.
b. 3M Company
c. BNSF Railway
d. Comprehensive income

20. The _____ is the former authoritative body of the American Institute of Certified Public Accountants (AICPA.) It was created by the American Institute of Certified Public Accountants in 1959 and issued pronouncements on accounting principles until 1973, when it was replaced by the Financial Accounting Standards Board (FASB.)

The _____ was disbanded in the hopes that the smaller, fully-independent FASB could more effectively create accounting standards.

a. Institute of Management Accountants
b. International Federation of Accountants
c. American Payroll Association
d. Accounting Principles Board

21. _____ in economics and business is the result of an exchange and from that trade we assign a numerical monetary value to a good, service or asset. If Alice trades Bob 4 apples for an orange, the _____ of an orange is 4 apples. Inversely, the _____ of an apple is 1/4 oranges.

a. Transactional Net Margin Method
b. Discounts and allowances
c. Price discrimination
d. Price

22. _____ are sometimes the same as net worth, or shareholders' equity - assets minus liabilities. The term _____ is commonly used with charities or not for profit entities. Although these entities don't make money, it is important to maintain reasonable reserves to help future growth.

a. Net assets
b. Sortino ratio
c. Net interest spread
d. Debtor days

23. _____ are defined as identifiable non-monetary assets that cannot be seen, touched or physically measured, which are created through time and/or effort and that are identifiable as a separate asset. There are two primary forms of intangibles - legal intangibles (such as trade secrets (e.g., customer lists), copyrights, patents, trademarks, and goodwill) and competitive intangibles (such as knowledge activities (know-how, knowledge), collaboration activities, leverage activities, and structural activities.) Legal intangibles are known under the generic term intellectual property and generate legal property rights defensible in a court of law.

Chapter 1. Intercorporate Acquisitions and Investments in Other Entities

a. AIG
b. ABC Television Network
c. Overhead
d. Intangible assets

24. _____ refers to a business or organization attempting to acquire goods or services to accomplish the goals of the enterprise. Though there are several organizations that attempt to set standards in the _____ process, processes can vary greatly between organizations. Typically the word e;_____e; is not used interchangeably with the word e;procuremente;, since procurement typically includes Expediting, Supplier Quality, and Traffic and Logistics (T'L) in addition to _____.

a. Supply chain
b. Consignor
c. Free port
d. Purchasing

25. _____ means the giving out of information, either voluntarily or to be in compliance with legal regulations or workplace rules.

- In Computer security, full _____ means disclosing full information about vulnerabilities.
- In computing, _____ widget
- Journalism, full _____ refers to disclosing the interests of the writer which may bear on the subject being written about, for example, if the writer has worked with an interview subject in the past.

- In law:
    - The law of England and Wales, _____ refers to a process that may form part of legal proceedings, whereby parties inform to other parties the existence of any relevant documents that are, or have been, in their control. This compares with the process known as discovery in the course of legal proceedings in the United States.
    - In U.S. civil procedure (litigation rules for civil cases), _____ is a stage prior to trial. In civil cases, each party must disclose to the opposing party the following: names of witnesses which it may use to support its side, copies of documents (or mere description of these documents) in its control which it may use to support its side, computation of damages claimed, and certain insurance information. _____ is related to, but technically prior to, the discovery stage.
    - In Company law (known as 'corporate law' in the United States), _____ refers to giving out information about public or limited companies or their officers, which might be kept secret if the company was a private company or a partnership.

- In real property transactions, _____ refers to providing to a buyer information known to the seller or broker/agent concerning the condition or other aspects of real property that would affect the property's value or desirability. These rules regarding what information must be disclosed, and whether the information must be disclosed even if a buyer does not ask, vary from one jurisdiction to the next.

a. Tax harmonisation
b. Controlled Foreign Corporations
c. Trailing
d. Disclosure

26. Most patent law systems require that a patent application disclose a claimed invention in sufficient detail for the notional person skilled in the art to carry out that claimed invention. This requirement is often known as sufficiency of disclosure or enablement, depending on the jurisdiction.

The _____ lies at the heart and origin of patent law. A state or government grants an inventor, or the inventor's assignee, a monopoly for a given period of time in exchange for the inventor disclosing to the public how to make or practice his or her invention. If a patent fails to contain such information, then the bargain is violated, and the patent is unenforceable.

a. Tax patent
b. False Claims Act
c. Disclosure requirement
d. Pre-emption right

Chapter 2. Reporting Intercorporate Interests

1. _____, formerly part of AT'T Corp., was a wireless telephone carrier in the United States, based in Redmond, Washington, and later traded on the New York Stock Exchange under the stock symbol 'AWE', as a separate entity from its former parent.

On October 26, 2004, AT'T Wireless completed a merger with Cingular Wireless, a joint venture of SBC Communications and BellSouth, to become the largest wireless carrier in the United States. Under the agreement, only the Cingular brand name would remain.

  a. Amgen
  b. AT'T Wireless Services, Inc.
  c. Allstate Corporation
  d. AIG

2. A _____ is a company that owns enough voting stock in another firm to control management and operations by influencing or electing its board of directors; the second company being deemed as a subsidiary of the _____. The definition of a _____ differs from jurisdiction to jurisdiction, with the definition normally being defined by way of laws dealing with companies in that jurisdiction.

The _____-subsidiary company relationship is defined by Part 1.2, Division 6, Section 46 of the Corporations Act 2001 (Cth), which states:

A body corporate (in this section called the first body) is a subsidiary of another body corporate if, and only if:

  (a) the other body:

  (i) controls the composition of the first body's board; or

  (ii) is in a position to cast, or control the casting of, more than one-half of the maximum number of votes that might be cast at a general meeting of the first body; or

  (iii) holds more than one-half of the issued share capital of the first body (excluding any part of that issued share capital that carries no right to participate beyond a specified amount in a distribution of either profits or capital); or

  (b) the first body is a subsidiary of a subsidiary of the other body.

  a. Subsidiary
  b. 3M Company
  c. BMC Software, Inc.
  d. Parent company

3. A _____, in business matters, is an entity that is controlled by a bigger and more powerful entity. The controlled entity is called a company, corporation, or limited liability company, and the controlling entity is called its parent (or the parent company.) The reason for this distinction is that a lone company cannot be a _____ of any organization; only an entity representing a legal fiction as a separate entity can be a _____.

  a. BMC Software, Inc.
  b. Subsidiary
  c. Parent company
  d. 3M Company

Chapter 2. Reporting Intercorporate Interests

4. In accounting/accountancy, _____ are journal entries usually made at the end of an accounting period to allocate income and expenditure to the period in which they actually occurred. The revenue recognition principle is the basis of making _____ that pertain to unearned and accrued revenues under accrual-basis accounting. They are sometimes called Balance Day adjustments because they are made on balance day.

   a. Accrued expense
   b. Adjusting entries
   c. Earnings before interest, taxes, depreciation and amortization
   d. Accrual

5. _____ is a form of corporation equity ownership represented in the securities. It is a stock whose dividends are based on market fluctuations. It is dangerous in comparison to preferred shares and some other investment options, in that in the event of bankruptcy, _____ investors receive their funds after preferred stock holders, bondholders, creditors, etc. On the other hand, common shares on average perform better than preferred shares or bonds over time.

   a. Stock split
   b. 3M Company
   c. Growth investing
   d. Common stock

6. _____ is a specific term used in companies' financial reporting from the company-whole point of view. Because that use excludes the effects of changing ownership interest, an economic measure of _____ is necessary for financial analysis from the shareholders' point of view

   _____ is defined by the Financial Accounting Standards Board, or FASB, as 'the change in equity [net assets] of a business enterprise during a period from transactions and other events and circumstances from nonowner sources. It includes all changes in equity during a period except those resulting from investments by owners and distributions to owners.'

   _____ is the sum of net income and other items that must bypass the income statement because they have not been realized, including items like an unrealized holding gain or loss from available for sale securities and foreign currency translation gains or losses.

   a. BNSF Railway
   b. BMC Software, Inc.
   c. Comprehensive income
   d. 3M Company

7. In economics, business, retail, and accounting, a _____ is the value of money that has been used up to produce something, and hence is not available for use anymore. In economics, a _____ is an alternative that is given up as a result of a decision. In business, the _____ may be one of acquisition, in which case the amount of money expended to acquire it is counted as _____.

   a. Cost of quality
   b. Cost
   c. Cost allocation
   d. Prime cost

8. _____ is that which is owed; usually referencing assets owed, but the term can also cover moral obligations and other interactions not requiring money. In the case of assets, _____ is a means of using future purchasing power in the present before a summation has been earned. Some companies and corporations use _____ as a part of their overall corporate finance strategy.

   a. Loan
   b. Lender
   c. Debenture
   d. Debt

Chapter 2. Reporting Intercorporate Interests

9. _____ in accounting is the process of treating equity investments, usually 20-50%, in associate companies. The investor keeps such equities as an asset. Proportional share of associate company's net income increases the investment, and proportional payment of dividends decreases it.
   a. Out-of-pocket
   b. ABC Television Network
   c. AIG
   d. Equity method

10. The _____ is a private, not-for-profit organization whose primary purpose is to develop generally accepted accounting principles (GAAP) within the United States in the public's interest. The Securities and Exchange Commission (SEC) designated the _____ as the organization responsible for setting accounting standards for public companies in the U.S. It was created in 1973, replacing the Accounting Principles Board and the Committee on Accounting Procedure of the American Institute of Certified Public Accountants. The _____'s mission is 'to establish and improve standards of financial accounting and reporting for the guidance and education of the public, including issuers, auditors, and users of financial information.'

    The _____ is not a governmental body.

    a. Fannie Mae
    b. Public company
    c. Governmental Accounting Standards Board
    d. Financial Accounting Standards Board

11. A _____ is a fungible, negotiable instrument representing financial value. they are broadly categorized into debt securities (such as banknotes, bonds and debentures), and equity securities; e.g., common stocks. The company or other entity issuing the _____ is called the issuer.
    a. Security
    b. Tracking stock
    c. 3M Company
    d. BMC Software, Inc.

12. _____ are payments made by a corporation to its shareholder members. It is the portion of corporate profits paid out to stockholders. When a corporation earns a profit or surplus, that money can be put to two uses: it can either be re-invested in the business (called retained earnings), or it can be paid to the shareholders as a dividend.
    a. Dividend stripping
    b. Dividends
    c. Dividend yield
    d. Dividend payout ratio

13. _____ is a payment of a dividend to stockholders that exceeds the company's retained earnings. Once retained earnings is depleted, capital accounts such as additional paid-in capital are decreased to make up for the remaining dividend to be paid to stockholders. When a _____ occurs, it is considered to be a return of investment instead of profits.
    a. Liquidating dividend
    b. Trade name
    c. Redemption value
    d. Fund accounting

14. An _____ is the buying of one company by another. An _____ may be friendly or hostile. In the former case, the companies cooperate in negotiations; in the latter case, the takeover target is unwilling to be bought or the target's board has no prior knowledge of the offer. _____ usually refers to a purchase of a smaller firm by a larger one. Sometimes, however, a smaller firm will acquire management control of a larger or longer established company and keep its name for the combined entity. This is known as a reverse takeover.
    a. Acquisition
    b. ABC Television Network
    c. AMEX
    d. AIG

Chapter 2. Reporting Intercorporate Interests

15. The _____ is the former authoritative body of the American Institute of Certified Public Accountants (AICPA.) It was created by the American Institute of Certified Public Accountants in 1959 and issued pronouncements on accounting principles until 1973, when it was replaced by the Financial Accounting Standards Board (FASB.)

The _____ was disbanded in the hopes that the smaller, fully-independent FASB could more effectively create accounting standards.

a. Accounting Principles Board
b. Institute of Management Accountants
c. American Payroll Association
d. International Federation of Accountants

16. A _____ is an entity formed between two or more parties to undertake economic activity together. The parties agree to create a new entity by both contributing equity, and they then share in the revenues, expenses, and control of the enterprise. The venture can be for one specific project only, or a continuing business relationship such as the Fuji Xerox _____.

a. Fraud Enforcement and Recovery Act
b. Chief Financial Officers Act of 1990
c. Pre-emption right
d. Joint venture

17. _____ of something is, in finance, the adding together of interest or different investments over a period of time such as atoms (1 - the act or process of accruing; 2 - the amount that accrues.) It holds specific meanings in accounting and payroll.

_____, in accounting, describes the accounting method known as _____ basis, whereby revenues and expenses are recognized when they are accrued, i.e. accumulated (earned or incurred), regardless when the actual cash is received or paid out.

a. Accounts receivable
b. Assets
c. Earnings before interest, taxes, depreciation and amortization
d. Accrual

18. _____ is the process of increasing, or accounting for, an amount over a period of time. Particular instances of the term include:

- _____, the allocation of a lump sum amount to different time periods, particularly for loans and other forms of finance, including related interest or other finance charges.
    - _____ schedule, a table detailing each periodic payment on a loan (typically a mortgage), as generated by an _____ calculator.
    - Negative _____, an _____ schedule where the loan amount actually increases through not paying the full interest
- Amortized analysis, analyzing the execution cost of algorithms over a sequence of operations.
- _____ of capital expenditures of certain assets under accounting rules, particularly intangible assets, in a manner analogous to depreciation.
- _____

a. Amortization
b. Annuity
c. EBIT
d. Intangible

Chapter 2. Reporting Intercorporate Interests

19. In accounting, _____ or carrying value is the value of an asset according to its balance sheet account balance. For assets, the value is based on the original cost of the asset less any depreciation, amortization or impairment costs made against the asset. Traditionally, a company's _____ is its total assets minus intangible assets and liabilities.
    a. Depreciation
    b. Generally accepted accounting principles
    c. Matching principle
    d. Book value

20. In business and accounting, _____ are everything of value that is owned by a person or company. It is a claim on the property your income of a borrower. The balance sheet of a firm records the monetary value of the _____ owned by the firm.
    a. Earnings before interest, taxes, depreciation and amortization
    b. Accrual basis accounting
    c. Accounts receivable
    d. Assets

21. _____ are defined as identifiable non-monetary assets that cannot be seen, touched or physically measured, which are created through time and/or effort and that are identifiable as a separate asset. There are two primary forms of intangibles - legal intangibles (such as trade secrets (e.g., customer lists), copyrights, patents, trademarks, and goodwill) and competitive intangibles (such as knowledge activities (know-how, knowledge), collaboration activities, leverage activities, and structural activities.) Legal intangibles are known under the generic term intellectual property and generate legal property rights defensible in a court of law.
    a. AIG
    b. ABC Television Network
    c. Overhead
    d. Intangible assets

22. A _____ is a type of business entity in which partners (owners) share with each other the profits or losses of the business undertaking in which all have invested. _____s are often favored over corporations for taxation purposes, as the _____ structure does not generally incur a tax on profits before it is distributed to the partners (i.e. there is no dividend tax levied.) However, depending on the _____ structure and the jurisdiction in which it operates, owners of a _____ may be exposed to greater personal liability than they would as shareholders of a corporation.
    a. Corporate governance
    b. National Information Infrastructure Protection Act
    c. Resource Conservation and Recovery Act
    d. Partnership

23. _____ were documents issued by the Committee on Accounting Procedure between 1938 and 1959 on various accounting problems. They were discontinued with the dissolution of the Committee in 1959 under a recommendation from the Special Committee on Research Program. In all, 51 bulletins were issued, however, the lack of binding authority over AICPA's membership reduced the influence of, and compliance with the content of the bulletins.
    a. ABC Television Network
    b. Other postemployment benefits
    c. AIG
    d. Accounting Research Bulletins

24. _____ are financial statements that factor the holding company's subsidiaries into its aggregated accounting figure. It is a representation of how the holding company is doing as a group. The consolidated accounts should provide a true and fair view of the financial and operating conditions of the group.
    a. Replacement cost
    b. Committee on Accounting Procedure
    c. Redemption value
    d. Consolidated financial statements

Chapter 2. Reporting Intercorporate Interests

25. _____, revised and replaced in its entirety by FIN 46R, is a statement for the purposes of United States Generally Accepted Accounting Principles published by the US Financial Accounting Standards Board (FASB) which requires a reporting enterprise to consolidate a variable interest entity (VIE) if it is the primary beneficiary of the VIE based on variable interests. One of the main reasons FIN46 was issued as an interpretation instead of an accounting standard was to issue the standard in a relatively short period of time in response to the Enron scandal.

FIN 46R is an interpretation of ARB 51 relating to consolidation.

- a. BMC Software, Inc.
- c. BNSF Railway
- b. 3M Company
- d. FIN 46

26. _____ are formal records of a business' financial activities.

In British English, including United Kingdom company law, _____ are often referred to as accounts, although the term _____ is also used, particularly by accountants.

_____ provide an overview of a business' financial condition in both short and long term.

- a. Notes to the financial statements
- c. Statement of retained earnings
- b. 3M Company
- d. Financial Statements

27. _____ is a fee paid on borrowed assets. It is the price paid for the use of borrowed money , or, money earned by deposited funds .Assets that are sometimes lent with _____ include money, shares, consumer goods through hire purchase, major assets such as aircraft, and even entire factories in finance lease arrangements. The _____ is calculated upon the value of the assets in the same manner as upon money.
- a. Interest
- c. AIG
- b. Insolvency
- d. ABC Television Network

28. _____ is generally understood in financial circles as the point at which revenue is recognized, typically through a transaction which involves the exchange of an asset, product, or service for cash or its equivalents.

This approach gives the accounting division a strictly objective basis for changing the books. For example, a homeowner may believe that his house has grown in value during a strong market, or fallen in value during a weak market, but until the house is actually sold for a specific price to a specific buyer, the change in value can only be estimated and is considered unrealized.

- a. Realization
- c. Valuation
- b. Merck ' Co., Inc.
- d. Total-factor productivity

29. An _____ is a tax levied on the financial income of people, corporations, or other legal entities. Various _____ systems exist, with varying degrees of tax incidence. Income taxation can be progressive, proportional, or regressive.
- a. Income Tax
- c. Individual Retirement Arrangement
- b. Implied level of government service
- d. Ordinary income

Chapter 2. Reporting Intercorporate Interests

30. In accounting, _____ has a very specific meaning. It is an outflow of cash or other valuable assets from a person or company to another person or company. This outflow of cash is generally one side of a trade for products or services that have equal or better current or future value to the buyer than to the seller.

   a. AMEX
   c. ABC Television Network
   b. AIG
   d. Expense

31. At its simplest, a company's _____ as it sometimes called, is computed in by multiplying the income before tax number, as reported to shareholders, by the appropriate tax rate. In reality, the computation is typically considerably more complex due to things such as expenses considered not deductible by taxing authorities ('add backs'), the range of tax rates applicable to various levels of income, different tax rates in different jurisdictions, multiple layers of tax on income, and other issues.

Historically, in many places, a revenue-expense method was used, in which the income statement was seen as primary, and the balance sheet as secondary.

   a. Payroll
   c. Total Expense Ratio
   b. 3M Company
   d. Tax expense

Chapter 3. The Reporting Entity and Consolidated Financial Statements

1. _____ are financial statements that factor the holding company's subsidiaries into its aggregated accounting figure. It is a representation of how the holding company is doing as a group. The consolidated accounts should provide a true and fair view of the financial and operating conditions of the group.
   - a. Redemption value
   - b. Replacement cost
   - c. Committee on Accounting Procedure
   - d. Consolidated financial statements

2. _____ are formal records of a business' financial activities.

   In British English, including United Kingdom company law, _____ are often referred to as accounts, although the term _____ is also used, particularly by accountants.

   _____ provide an overview of a business' financial condition in both short and long term.

   - a. 3M Company
   - b. Notes to the financial statements
   - c. Financial statements
   - d. Statement of retained earnings

3. A _____, in business matters, is an entity that is controlled by a bigger and more powerful entity. The controlled entity is called a company, corporation, or limited liability company, and the controlling entity is called its parent (or the parent company.) The reason for this distinction is that a lone company cannot be a _____ of any organization; only an entity representing a legal fiction as a separate entity can be a _____.
   - a. Parent company
   - b. 3M Company
   - c. BMC Software, Inc.
   - d. Subsidiary

4. _____ were documents issued by the Committee on Accounting Procedure between 1938 and 1959 on various accounting problems. They were discontinued with the dissolution of the Committee in 1959 under a recommendation from the Special Committee on Research Program. In all, 51 bulletins were issued, however, the lack of binding authority over AICPA's membership reduced the influence of, and compliance with the content of the bulletins.
   - a. AIG
   - b. ABC Television Network
   - c. Other postemployment benefits
   - d. Accounting Research Bulletins

5. The _____ is a private, not-for-profit organization whose primary purpose is to develop generally accepted accounting principles (GAAP) within the United States in the public's interest. The Securities and Exchange Commission (SEC) designated the _____ as the organization responsible for setting accounting standards for public companies in the U.S. It was created in 1973, replacing the Accounting Principles Board and the Committee on Accounting Procedure of the American Institute of Certified Public Accountants. The _____'s mission is 'to establish and improve standards of financial accounting and reporting for the guidance and education of the public, including issuers, auditors, and users of financial information.'

   The _____ is not a governmental body.

   - a. Fannie Mae
   - b. Public company
   - c. Governmental Accounting Standards Board
   - d. Financial Accounting Standards Board

Chapter 3. The Reporting Entity and Consolidated Financial Statements

6. The term _____ refers to government debt, expenditures and revenues, or to finance (particularly financial revenue) in general.

- _____ deficit is the budget deficit of federal or local government
- _____ policy is the discretionary spending of governments. Contrasts with monetary policy.
- _____ year and _____ quarter are reporting periods for firms and other agencies.

See also

- Procurator _____ and Crown Office and Procurator _____ Service

a. Swap
b. Fiscal
c. Comparable
d. Scientific Research and Experimental Development Tax Incentive Program

7. The _____ is currently the source of generally accepted accounting principles (GAAP) used by State and Local governments in the [[United States of America]]. As with most of the entities involved in creating GAAP in the United States, it is a private, non-governmental organization.

The _____ is subject to oversight by the Financial Accounting Foundation (FAF), which selects the members of the _____ and the Financial Accounting Standards Board, and funds both organizations.

a. National Conference of Commissioners on Uniform State Laws
b. Multinational corporation
c. Fannie Mae
d. Governmental Accounting Standards Board

8. In monetary economics _____ can refer either to a particular _____, for example British Pounds or United States Dollars, or, to the coins and banknotes of a particular _____, which actually form only a small part of the monetary base of a nation's money supply. The other part of a nation's money supply consists of money deposited in banks (sometimes called deposit money), ownership of which can be transferred by means of checks (cheques in the United Kingdom and Australia) or other forms of money transfer such as credit and debit cards. Deposit money and _____ are 'money' in the sense that both are acceptable as a means of exchange, but money need not necessarily be '_____'.

a. Currency
b. BNSF Railway
c. 3M Company
d. BMC Software, Inc.

9. In business and accounting, _____ are everything of value that is owned by a person or company. It is a claim on the property your income of a borrower. The balance sheet of a firm records the monetary value of the _____ owned by the firm.

a. Accounts receivable
b. Accrual basis accounting
c. Assets
d. Earnings before interest, taxes, depreciation and amortization

Chapter 3. The Reporting Entity and Consolidated Financial Statements 17

10. _____ (or _____ Financial Services), formerly known as _____, is a United States bank that was previously the wholly owned financial services arm of General Motors. _____ Financial Services provide a suite of financial programs including insurance and mortgage operations in approximately 40 countries around the world. In 2008, the firm provided financing to 75 percent of the 6,450 GM dealers.
   a. GMAC
   b. BMC Software, Inc.
   c. 3M Company
   d. BNSF Railway

11. In financial accounting, a _____ is defined as an obligation of an entity arising from past transactions or events, the settlement of which may result in the transfer or use of assets, provision of services or other yielding of economic benefits in the future.
   a. Vested
   b. Corporate governance
   c. False Claims Act
   d. Liability

12. _____ is a form of corporation equity ownership represented in the securities. It is a stock whose dividends are based on market fluctuations. It is dangerous in comparison to preferred shares and some other investment options, in that in the event of bankruptcy, _____ investors receive their funds after preferred stock holders, bondholders, creditors, etc. On the other hand, common shares on average perform better than preferred shares or bonds over time.
   a. 3M Company
   b. Growth investing
   c. Stock split
   d. Common stock

13. In accounting, _____ or carrying value is the value of an asset according to its balance sheet account balance. For assets, the value is based on the original cost of the asset less any depreciation, amortization or impairment costs made against the asset. Traditionally, a company's _____ is its total assets minus intangible assets and liabilities.
   a. Matching principle
   b. Generally accepted accounting principles
   c. Depreciation
   d. Book value

14. In economics, business, retail, and accounting, a _____ is the value of money that has been used up to produce something, and hence is not available for use anymore. In economics, a _____ is an alternative that is given up as a result of a decision. In business, the _____ may be one of acquisition, in which case the amount of money expended to acquire it is counted as _____.
   a. Cost allocation
   b. Cost of quality
   c. Prime cost
   d. Cost

15. A _____ is the pinnacle activity involved in selling products or services in return for money or other compensation. It is an act of completion of a commercial activity.

    A _____ is completed by the seller, the owner of the goods.

   a. Maturity
   b. Tertiary sector of economy
   c. High yield stock
   d. Sale

16. In finance, a _____ is a debt security, in which the authorized issuer owes the holders a debt and, depending on the terms of the _____, is obliged to pay interest (the coupon) and/or to repay the principal at a later date, termed maturity. It is a formal contract to repay borrowed money with interest at fixed intervals.

Chapter 3. The Reporting Entity and Consolidated Financial Statements

Thus a _____ is like a loan: the issuer is the borrower, the _____ holder is the lender, and the coupon is the interest.

a. Revenue bonds
b. Bond
c. Coupon rate
d. Zero-coupon bond

17. _____ is a fee paid on borrowed assets. It is the price paid for the use of borrowed money, or, money earned by deposited funds. Assets that are sometimes lent with _____ include money, shares, consumer goods through hire purchase, major assets such as aircraft, and even entire factories in finance lease arrangements. The _____ is calculated upon the value of the assets in the same manner as upon money.

a. Interest
b. Insolvency
c. AIG
d. ABC Television Network

18. _____ in business is an accounting concept that refers to ownership of a company (subsidiary) that is less than 50% of outstanding shares. _____ belongs to other investors and is reported on the consolidated balance sheet of the owning company to reflect the claim on assets belonging to other, non-controlling shareholders. Also, _____ is reported on the consolidated income statement as a share of profit belonging to minority shareholders.

a. Subledger
b. Bankruptcy prediction
c. Minority interest
d. Credit memo

19. _____ is an adverb or adjective, meaning in proportion. The term is used in many legal and economic contexts, and sometimes spelled pro-rata.

More specifically, _____ means:

1. In proportion to some factor that can be exactly calculated.
2. To count based on amount of time that has passed out of the total time.
3. Proportional Ratio

Pro-rata has a Latin etymology, from pro, according to, for, or by, and rata, feminine ablative of calculated.

Examples in law and economics include the following noted below.

a. BNSF Railway
b. BMC Software, Inc.
c. 3M Company
d. Pro rata

20. The word _____ indicates that a party, or proprietor, exercises private ownership, control or use over an item of property

a. BNSF Railway
b. BMC Software, Inc.
c. 3M Company
d. Proprietary

21. In accounting/accountancy, _____ are journal entries usually made at the end of an accounting period to allocate income and expenditure to the period in which they actually occurred. The revenue recognition principle is the basis of making _____ that pertain to unearned and accrued revenues under accrual-basis accounting. They are sometimes called Balance Day adjustments because they are made on balance day.

Chapter 3. The Reporting Entity and Consolidated Financial Statements 19

a. Earnings before interest, taxes, depreciation and amortization

b. Accrued expense

c. Accrual

d. Adjusting entries

22. _____ is a specific term used in companies' financial reporting from the company-whole point of view. Because that use excludes the effects of changing ownership interest, an economic measure of _____ is necessary for financial analysis from the shareholders' point of view

_____ is defined by the Financial Accounting Standards Board, or FASB, as 'the change in equity [net assets] of a business enterprise during a period from transactions and other events and circumstances from nonowner sources. It includes all changes in equity during a period except those resulting from investments by owners and distributions to owners.'

_____ is the sum of net income and other items that must bypass the income statement because they have not been realized, including items like an unrealized holding gain or loss from available for sale securities and foreign currency translation gains or losses.

a. 3M Company

b. Comprehensive income

c. BNSF Railway

d. BMC Software, Inc.

23. A _____ is a company that owns enough voting stock in another firm to control management and operations by influencing or electing its board of directors; the second company being deemed as a subsidiary of the _____. The definition of a _____ differs from jurisdiction to jurisdiction, with the definition normally being defined by way of laws dealing with companies in that jurisdiction.

The _____-subsidiary company relationship is defined by Part 1.2, Division 6, Section 46 of the Corporations Act 2001 (Cth), which states:

A body corporate (in this section called the first body) is a subsidiary of another body corporate if, and only if:

(a) the other body:

(i) controls the composition of the first body's board; or

(ii) is in a position to cast, or control the casting of, more than one-half of the maximum number of votes that might be cast at a general meeting of the first body; or

(iii) holds more than one-half of the issued share capital of the first body (excluding any part of that issued share capital that carries no right to participate beyond a specified amount in a distribution of either profits or capital); or

(b) the first body is a subsidiary of a subsidiary of the other body.

a. 3M Company
b. Subsidiary
c. BMC Software, Inc.
d. Parent company

24. The _____ is the former authoritative body of the American Institute of Certified Public Accountants (AICPA.) It was created by the American Institute of Certified Public Accountants in 1959 and issued pronouncements on accounting principles until 1973, when it was replaced by the Financial Accounting Standards Board (FASB.)

The _____ was disbanded in the hopes that the smaller, fully-independent FASB could more effectively create accounting standards.

   a. International Federation of Accountants
   b. Institute of Management Accountants
   c. American Payroll Association
   d. Accounting Principles Board

25. _____ in accounting is the process of treating equity investments, usually 20-50%, in associate companies. The investor keeps such equities as an asset. Proportional share of associate company's net income increases the investment, and proportional payment of dividends decreases it.
   a. Out-of-pocket
   b. ABC Television Network
   c. AIG
   d. Equity Method

Chapter 4. Consolidation as of the Date of Acquisition 21

1. An _____ is the buying of one company by another. An _____ may be friendly or hostile. In the former case, the companies cooperate in negotiations; in the latter case, the takeover target is unwilling to be bought or the target's board has no prior knowledge of the offer. _____ usually refers to a purchase of a smaller firm by a larger one. Sometimes, however, a smaller firm will acquire management control of a larger or longer established company and keep its name for the combined entity. This is known as a reverse takeover.

   a. ABC Television Network
   b. AIG
   c. AMEX
   d. Acquisition

2. In financial accounting, a _____ or statement of financial position is a summary of a person's or organization's balances. Assets, liabilities and ownership equity are listed as of a specific date, such as the end of its financial year. A _____ is often described as a snapshot of a company's financial condition.

   a. Statement of retained earnings
   b. Financial statements
   c. 3M Company
   d. Balance sheet

3. _____ is the state or fact of exclusive rights and control over property, which may be an object, land/real estate or intellectual property. An _____ right is also referred to as title.

   _____ is the key building block in the development of the capitalist socio-economic system.

   a. Administrative proceeding
   b. ABC Television Network
   c. Ownership
   d. Encumbrance

4. In accounting, _____ or carrying value is the value of an asset according to its balance sheet account balance. For assets, the value is based on the original cost of the asset less any depreciation, amortization or impairment costs made against the asset. Traditionally, a company's _____ is its total assets minus intangible assets and liabilities.

   a. Matching principle
   b. Depreciation
   c. Book value
   d. Generally accepted accounting principles

5. The _____ is a private, not-for-profit organization whose primary purpose is to develop generally accepted accounting principles (GAAP) within the United States in the public's interest. The Securities and Exchange Commission (SEC) designated the _____ as the organization responsible for setting accounting standards for public companies in the U.S. It was created in 1973, replacing the Accounting Principles Board and the Committee on Accounting Procedure of the American Institute of Certified Public Accountants. The _____'s mission is 'to establish and improve standards of financial accounting and reporting for the guidance and education of the public, including issuers, auditors, and users of financial information.'

   The _____ is not a governmental body.

   a. Fannie Mae
   b. Public company
   c. Governmental Accounting Standards Board
   d. Financial Accounting Standards Board

6. _____ and credit are formal bookkeeping and accounting terms. They are the most fundamental concepts in accounting, representing the two records that one party in a transaction makes on its records, transferring a money balance from one account to another, one representing a reduction of liability or increase in asset, and the other representing a balancing increase in liability or reduction of asset.

Introduction

_____s and credits are a system of notation used in accounting to keep track of money movements (transactions) into and out of an account.

a. Debit and credit
b. Debit
c. Cookie jar accounting
d. Bookkeeping

7. _____ refers to a business or organization attempting to acquire goods or services to accomplish the goals of the enterprise. Though there are several organizations that attempt to set standards in the _____ process, processes can vary greatly between organizations. Typically the word e;_____e; is not used interchangeably with the word e;procuremente;, since procurement typically includes Expediting, Supplier Quality, and Traffic and Logistics (T'L) in addition to _____.

a. Purchasing
b. Consignor
c. Free port
d. Supply chain

8. _____ in a corporation means to have control of a large enough block of voting stock shares in a company such that no one stock holder or coalition of stock holders can successfully oppose a motion. In theory this normally means that _____ would be 50% of the voting shares plus one.

In practice, though, _____ can be far less than that, as it is rare that 100% of a company's voting shareholders actively vote.

a. Participating preferred stock
b. Public offering
c. Controlling interest
d. Preferred stock

9. _____, also called fair price (in a commonplace conflation of the two distinct concepts), is a concept used in finance and economics, defined as a rational and unbiased estimate of the potential market price of a good, service, or asset, taking into account such objective factors as:

- acquisition/production/distribution costs, replacement costs, or costs of close substitutes
- actual utility at a given level of development of social productive capability
- supply vs. demand

and subjective factors such as

- risk characteristics
- cost of capital
- individually perceived utility

Chapter 4. Consolidation as of the Date of Acquisition

In accounting, _____ is used as an estimate of the market value of an asset (or liability) for which a market price cannot be determined (usually because there is no established market for the asset.) Under GAAP (FAS 157), _____ is the amount at which the asset could be bought or sold in a current transaction between willing parties, or transferred to an equivalent party, other than in a liquidation sale. This is used for assets whose carrying value is based on mark-to-market valuations; for assets carried at historical cost, the _____ of the asset is not used. One example of where _____ is an issue is a College kitchen with a cost of $2 million which was built 5 years ago.

a. 3M Company
c. BMC Software, Inc.
b. BNSF Railway
d. Fair value

10. _____ is a fee paid on borrowed assets. It is the price paid for the use of borrowed money , or, money earned by deposited funds .Assets that are sometimes lent with _____ include money, shares, consumer goods through hire purchase, major assets such as aircraft, and even entire factories in finance lease arrangements. The _____ is calculated upon the value of the assets in the same manner as upon money.

a. AIG
c. ABC Television Network
b. Insolvency
d. Interest

11. Book Value = Original Cost - _____

Book value at the end of year becomes book value at the beginning of next year. The asset is depreciated until the book value equals scrap value.

If the vehicle were to be sold and the sales price exceeded the depreciated value (net book value) then the excess would be considered a gain and subject to depreciation recapture.

a. AIG
c. AMEX
b. Accumulated depreciation
d. ABC Television Network

12. In business and accounting, _____ are everything of value that is owned by a person or company. It is a claim on the property your income of a borrower. The balance sheet of a firm records the monetary value of the _____ owned by the firm.

a. Assets
c. Accounts receivable
b. Earnings before interest, taxes, depreciation and amortization
d. Accrual basis accounting

13. In finance, _____ is the process of estimating the potential market value of a financial asset or liability. They can be done on assets (for example, investments in marketable securities such as stocks, options, business enterprises, or intangible assets such as patents and trademarks) or on liabilities (e.g., Bonds issued by a company.) A _____ is required in many contexts including investment analysis, capital budgeting, merger and acquisition transactions, financial reporting, taxable events to determine the proper tax liability, and in litigation.

a. Disclosure
c. Vyborg Appeal
b. Valuation
d. Daybook

Chapter 4. Consolidation as of the Date of Acquisition

14. _____ is that which is owed; usually referencing assets owed, but the term can also cover moral obligations and other interactions not requiring money. In the case of assets, _____ is a means of using future purchasing power in the present before a summation has been earned. Some companies and corporations use _____ as a part of their overall corporate finance strategy.
   a. Loan
   b. Lender
   c. Debenture
   d. Debt

15. In financial accounting, a _____ is defined as an obligation of an entity arising from past transactions or events, the settlement of which may result in the transfer or use of assets, provision of services or other yielding of economic benefits in the future.
   a. Liability
   b. False Claims Act
   c. Corporate governance
   d. Vested

16. A _____ is a fungible, negotiable instrument representing financial value. they are broadly categorized into debt securities (such as banknotes, bonds and debentures), and equity securities; e.g., common stocks. The company or other entity issuing the _____ is called the issuer.
   a. 3M Company
   b. Tracking stock
   c. BMC Software, Inc.
   d. Security

17. _____ is a term used in accounting, economics and finance to spread the cost of an asset over the span of several years.

In simple words we can say that _____ is the reduction in the value of an asset due to usage, passage of time, wear and tear, technological outdating or obsolescence, depletion, inadequacy, rot, rust, decay or other such factors.

In accounting, _____ is a term used to describe any method of attributing the historical or purchase cost of an asset across its useful life, roughly corresponding to normal wear and tear.

   a. Net profit
   b. Current asset
   c. Depreciation
   d. General ledger

18. The _____ is the national, professional association of CPAs in the United States, with more than 330,000 members, including CPAs in business and industry, public practice, government, and education; student affiliates; and international associates. It sets ethical standards for the profession and U.S. auditing standards for audits of private companies; federal, state and local governments; and non-profit organizations.

Approximately 40% of its members are engaged in the practice of public accounting, in areas such as auditing, accounting, taxation, general business consulting, business valuation, personal financial planning and business technology.

   a. AIG
   b. ABC Television Network
   c. Other postemployment benefits
   d. American Institute of Certified Public Accountants

19. _____ are securities that can be easily converted into cash. Such securities will generally have highly liquid markets allowing the security to be sold at a reasonable price very quickly. This is a usual feature in real estate.

a. Marketable
b. 3M Company
c. BMC Software, Inc.
d. Tracking stock

20. Discounting is a financial mechanism in which a debtor obtains the right to delay payments to a creditor, for a defined period of time, in exchange for a charge or fee. Essentially, the party that owes money in the present purchases the right to delay the payment until some future date. The _____, or charge, is simply the difference between the original amount owed in the present and the amount that has to be paid in the future to settle the debt.

a. Discount factor
b. Risk aversion
c. Discount
d. Discounting

21. _____ is a specific term used in companies' financial reporting from the company-whole point of view. Because that use excludes the effects of changing ownership interest, an economic measure of _____ is necessary for financial analysis from the shareholders' point of view

_____ is defined by the Financial Accounting Standards Board, or FASB, as 'the change in equity [net assets] of a business enterprise during a period from transactions and other events and circumstances from nonowner sources. It includes all changes in equity during a period except those resulting from investments by owners and distributions to owners.'

_____ is the sum of net income and other items that must bypass the income statement because they have not been realized, including items like an unrealized holding gain or loss from available for sale securities and foreign currency translation gains or losses.

a. Comprehensive income
b. 3M Company
c. BNSF Railway
d. BMC Software, Inc.

22. A _____, in business matters, is an entity that is controlled by a bigger and more powerful entity. The controlled entity is called a company, corporation, or limited liability company, and the controlling entity is called its parent (or the parent company.) The reason for this distinction is that a lone company cannot be a _____ of any organization; only an entity representing a legal fiction as a separate entity can be a _____.

a. Parent company
b. BMC Software, Inc.
c. Subsidiary
d. 3M Company

Chapter 5. Consolidation Following Acquisition

1. An _____ is the buying of one company by another. An _____ may be friendly or hostile. In the former case, the companies cooperate in negotiations; in the latter case, the takeover target is unwilling to be bought or the target's board has no prior knowledge of the offer. _____ usually refers to a purchase of a smaller firm by a larger one. Sometimes, however, a smaller firm will acquire management control of a larger or longer established company and keep its name for the combined entity. This is known as a reverse takeover.

   a. AMEX
   b. ABC Television Network
   c. AIG
   d. Acquisition

2. _____ is equal to the income that a firm has after subtracting costs and expenses from the total revenue. _____ can be distributed among holders of common stock as a dividend or held by the firm as retained earnings.

   The items deducted will typically include tax expense, financing expense (interest expense), and minority interest. Likewise, preferred stock dividends will be subtracted too, though they are not an expense.

   a. Long-term liabilities
   b. Generally accepted accounting principles
   c. Matching principle
   d. Net income

3. _____ is a specific term used in companies' financial reporting from the company-whole point of view. Because that use excludes the effects of changing ownership interest, an economic measure of _____ is necessary for financial analysis from the shareholders' point of view

   _____ is defined by the Financial Accounting Standards Board, or FASB, as 'the change in equity [net assets] of a business enterprise during a period from transactions and other events and circumstances from nonowner sources. It includes all changes in equity during a period except those resulting from investments by owners and distributions to owners.'

   _____ is the sum of net income and other items that must bypass the income statement because they have not been realized, including items like an unrealized holding gain or loss from available for sale securities and foreign currency translation gains or losses.

   a. Comprehensive income
   b. 3M Company
   c. BMC Software, Inc.
   d. BNSF Railway

4. _____ is the state or fact of exclusive rights and control over property, which may be an object, land/real estate or intellectual property. An _____ right is also referred to as title.

   _____ is the key building block in the development of the capitalist socio-economic system.

   a. ABC Television Network
   b. Encumbrance
   c. Administrative proceeding
   d. Ownership

5. In accounting, _____ or carrying value is the value of an asset according to its balance sheet account balance. For assets, the value is based on the original cost of the asset less any depreciation, amortization or impairment costs made against the asset. Traditionally, a company's _____ is its total assets minus intangible assets and liabilities.

   a. Book value
   b. Depreciation
   c. Generally accepted accounting principles
   d. Matching principle

Chapter 5. Consolidation Following Acquisition

6. _____ in a corporation means to have control of a large enough block of voting stock shares in a company such that no one stock holder or coalition of stock holders can successfully oppose a motion. In theory this normally means that _____ would be 50% of the voting shares plus one.

In practice, though, _____ can be far less than that, as it is rare that 100% of a company's voting shareholders actively vote.

a. Public offering
b. Preferred stock
c. Participating preferred stock
d. Controlling interest

7. _____ is a fee paid on borrowed assets. It is the price paid for the use of borrowed money, or, money earned by deposited funds. Assets that are sometimes lent with _____ include money, shares, consumer goods through hire purchase, major assets such as aircraft, and even entire factories in finance lease arrangements. The _____ is calculated upon the value of the assets in the same manner as upon money.

a. ABC Television Network
b. AIG
c. Insolvency
d. Interest

8. _____ are financial statements that factor the holding company's subsidiaries into its aggregated accounting figure. It is a representation of how the holding company is doing as a group. The consolidated accounts should provide a true and fair view of the financial and operating conditions of the group.

a. Redemption value
b. Replacement cost
c. Committee on Accounting Procedure
d. Consolidated financial statements

9. The _____ is a private, not-for-profit organization whose primary purpose is to develop generally accepted accounting principles (GAAP) within the United States in the public's interest. The Securities and Exchange Commission (SEC) designated the _____ as the organization responsible for setting accounting standards for public companies in the U.S. It was created in 1973, replacing the Accounting Principles Board and the Committee on Accounting Procedure of the American Institute of Certified Public Accountants. The _____'s mission is 'to establish and improve standards of financial accounting and reporting for the guidance and education of the public, including issuers, auditors, and users of financial information.'

The _____ is not a governmental body.

a. Public company
b. Fannie Mae
c. Governmental Accounting Standards Board
d. Financial Accounting Standards Board

10. _____ are formal records of a business' financial activities.

In British English, including United Kingdom company law, _____ are often referred to as accounts, although the term _____ is also used, particularly by accountants.

_____ provide an overview of a business' financial condition in both short and long term.

a. Statement of retained earnings
b. 3M Company
c. Notes to the financial statements
d. Financial statements

11. A _____ is a company that owns enough voting stock in another firm to control management and operations by influencing or electing its board of directors; the second company being deemed as a subsidiary of the _____. The definition of a _____ differs from jurisdiction to jurisdiction, with the definition normally being defined by way of laws dealing with companies in that jurisdiction.

The _____-subsidiary company relationship is defined by Part 1.2, Division 6, Section 46 of the Corporations Act 2001 (Cth), which states:

A body corporate (in this section called the first body) is a subsidiary of another body corporate if, and only if:

(a) the other body:

(i) controls the composition of the first body's board; or

(ii) is in a position to cast, or control the casting of, more than one-half of the maximum number of votes that might be cast at a general meeting of the first body; or

(iii) holds more than one-half of the issued share capital of the first body (excluding any part of that issued share capital that carries no right to participate beyond a specified amount in a distribution of either profits or capital); or

(b) the first body is a subsidiary of a subsidiary of the other body.

a. BMC Software, Inc.
b. 3M Company
c. Subsidiary
d. Parent company

12. In accounting/accountancy, _____ are journal entries usually made at the end of an accounting period to allocate income and expenditure to the period in which they actually occurred. The revenue recognition principle is the basis of making _____ that pertain to unearned and accrued revenues under accrual-basis accounting. They are sometimes called Balance Day adjustments because they are made on balance day.

a. Accrual
b. Earnings before interest, taxes, depreciation and amortization
c. Accrued expense
d. Adjusting entries

13. A _____, in business matters, is an entity that is controlled by a bigger and more powerful entity. The controlled entity is called a company, corporation, or limited liability company, and the controlling entity is called its parent (or the parent company.) The reason for this distinction is that a lone company cannot be a _____ of any organization; only an entity representing a legal fiction as a separate entity can be a _____.

a. Parent company
b. 3M Company
c. Subsidiary
d. BMC Software, Inc.

14. In business and accounting, _____ are everything of value that is owned by a person or company. It is a claim on the property your income of a borrower. The balance sheet of a firm records the monetary value of the _____ owned by the firm.

Chapter 5. Consolidation Following Acquisition

a. Accrual basis accounting

b. Accounts receivable

c. Assets

d. Earnings before interest, taxes, depreciation and amortization

15. In financial accounting, a _____ is defined as an obligation of an entity arising from past transactions or events, the settlement of which may result in the transfer or use of assets, provision of services or other yielding of economic benefits in the future.

a. Liability

b. Corporate governance

c. False Claims Act

d. Vested

16. In economics, business, retail, and accounting, a _____ is the value of money that has been used up to produce something, and hence is not available for use anymore. In economics, a _____ is an alternative that is given up as a result of a decision. In business, the _____ may be one of acquisition, in which case the amount of money expended to acquire it is counted as _____.

a. Cost of quality

b. Cost allocation

c. Prime cost

d. Cost

Chapter 6. Intercorporate Transfers: Noncurrent Assets

1. In business and accounting, _____ are everything of value that is owned by a person or company. It is a claim on the property your income of a borrower. The balance sheet of a firm records the monetary value of the _____ owned by the firm.

   a. Accounts receivable
   b. Accrual basis accounting
   c. Assets
   d. Earnings before interest, taxes, depreciation and amortization

2. _____, also known as property, plant, and equipment (PP&E), is a term used in accountancy for assets and property which cannot easily be converted into cash. This can be compared with current assets such as cash or bank accounts, which are described as liquid assets. In most cases, only tangible assets are referred to as fixed.

   a. Bankruptcy prediction
   b. Fixed asset
   c. Minority interest
   d. Subledger

3. _____ were documents issued by the Committee on Accounting Procedure between 1938 and 1959 on various accounting problems. They were discontinued with the dissolution of the Committee in 1959 under a recommendation from the Special Committee on Research Program. In all, 51 bulletins were issued, however, the lack of binding authority over AICPA's membership reduced the influence of, and compliance with the content of the bulletins.

   a. Other postemployment benefits
   b. AIG
   c. Accounting Research Bulletins
   d. ABC Television Network

4. _____ are financial statements that factor the holding company's subsidiaries into its aggregated accounting figure. It is a representation of how the holding company is doing as a group. The consolidated accounts should provide a true and fair view of the financial and operating conditions of the group.

   a. Replacement cost
   b. Redemption value
   c. Committee on Accounting Procedure
   d. Consolidated financial statements

5. _____ are formal records of a business' financial activities.

   In British English, including United Kingdom company law, _____ are often referred to as accounts, although the term _____ is also used, particularly by accountants.

   _____ provide an overview of a business' financial condition in both short and long term.

   a. Statement of retained earnings
   b. Notes to the financial statements
   c. 3M Company
   d. Financial Statements

6. _____ is generally understood in financial circles as the point at which revenue is recognized, typically through a transaction which involves the exchange of an asset, product, or service for cash or its equivalents.

   This approach gives the accounting division a strictly objective basis for changing the books. For example, a homeowner may believe that his house has grown in value during a strong market, or fallen in value during a weak market, but until the house is actually sold for a specific price to a specific buyer, the change in value can only be estimated and is considered unrealized.

   a. Merck ' Co., Inc.
   b. Total-factor productivity
   c. Valuation
   d. Realization

Chapter 6. Intercorporate Transfers: Noncurrent Assets

7. _____ means the giving out of information, either voluntarily or to be in compliance with legal regulations or workplace rules.

- In Computer security, full _____ means disclosing full information about vulnerabilities.
- In computing, _____ widget
- Journalism, full _____ refers to disclosing the interests of the writer which may bear on the subject being written about, for example, if the writer has worked with an interview subject in the past.

- In law:
    - The law of England and Wales, _____ refers to a process that may form part of legal proceedings, whereby parties inform to other parties the existence of any relevant documents that are, or have been, in their control. This compares with the process known as discovery in the course of legal proceedings in the United States.
    - In U.S. civil procedure (litigation rules for civil cases), _____ is a stage prior to trial. In civil cases, each party must disclose to the opposing party the following: names of witnesses which it may use to support its side, copies of documents (or mere description of these documents) in its control which it may use to support its side, computation of damages claimed, and certain insurance information. _____ is related to, but technically prior to, the discovery stage.
    - In Company law (known as 'corporate law' in the United States), _____ refers to giving out information about public or limited companies or their officers, which might be kept secret if the company was a private company or a partnership.

- In real property transactions, _____ refers to providing to a buyer information known to the seller or broker/agent concerning the condition or other aspects of real property that would affect the property's value or desirability. These rules regarding what information must be disclosed, and whether the information must be disclosed even if a buyer does not ask, vary from one jurisdiction to the next.

a. Tax harmonisation
b. Controlled Foreign Corporations
c. Trailing
d. Disclosure

8. A _____ is the pinnacle activity involved in selling products or services in return for money or other compensation. It is an act of completion of a commercial activity.

A _____ is completed by the seller, the owner of the goods.

a. Maturity
b. Sale
c. Tertiary sector of economy
d. High yield stock

9. _____ is equal to the income that a firm has after subtracting costs and expenses from the total revenue. _____ can be distributed among holders of common stock as a dividend or held by the firm as retained earnings.

The items deducted will typically include tax expense, financing expense (interest expense), and minority interest. Likewise, preferred stock dividends will be subtracted too, though they are not an expense.

a. Generally accepted accounting principles
c. Long-term liabilities
b. Matching principle
d. Net income

10. A _____ is a habit, a preparation, a state of readiness, or a tendency to act in a specified way.

The terms dispositional belief and occurrent belief refer, in the former case, to a belief that is held in the mind but not currently being considered, and in the latter case, to a belief that is currently being considered by the mind.

In Bourdieu's theory of fields _____s are the natural tendencies of each individual to take on a certain position in any field.

a. BMC Software, Inc.
c. BNSF Railway
b. 3M Company
d. Disposition

11. _____ is a specific term used in companies' financial reporting from the company-whole point of view. Because that use excludes the effects of changing ownership interest, an economic measure of _____ is necessary for financial analysis from the shareholders' point of view

_____ is defined by the Financial Accounting Standards Board, or FASB, as 'the change in equity [net assets] of a business enterprise during a period from transactions and other events and circumstances from nonowner sources. It includes all changes in equity during a period except those resulting from investments by owners and distributions to owners.'

_____ is the sum of net income and other items that must bypass the income statement because they have not been realized, including items like an unrealized holding gain or loss from available for sale securities and foreign currency translation gains or losses.

a. Comprehensive income
c. BNSF Railway
b. BMC Software, Inc.
d. 3M Company

12. _____ in accounting is the process of treating equity investments, usually 20-50%, in associate companies. The investor keeps such equities as an asset. Proportional share of associate company's net income increases the investment, and proportional payment of dividends decreases it.

a. Out-of-pocket
c. AIG
b. ABC Television Network
d. Equity method

13. In economics, business, retail, and accounting, a _____ is the value of money that has been used up to produce something, and hence is not available for use anymore. In economics, a _____ is an alternative that is given up as a result of a decision. In business, the _____ may be one of acquisition, in which case the amount of money expended to acquire it is counted as _____.

a. Cost of quality
c. Prime cost
b. Cost allocation
d. Cost

Chapter 7. Intercompany Inventory Transactions

1. In economics, business, retail, and accounting, a _____ is the value of money that has been used up to produce something, and hence is not available for use anymore. In economics, a _____ is an alternative that is given up as a result of a decision. In business, the _____ may be one of acquisition, in which case the amount of money expended to acquire it is counted as _____.

   a. Cost allocation
   b. Cost of quality
   c. Cost
   d. Prime cost

2. A _____ is the pinnacle activity involved in selling products or services in return for money or other compensation. It is an act of completion of a commercial activity.

   A _____ is completed by the seller, the owner of the goods.

   a. Maturity
   b. Tertiary sector of economy
   c. High yield stock
   d. Sale

3. _____ is equal to the income that a firm has after subtracting costs and expenses from the total revenue. _____ can be distributed among holders of common stock as a dividend or held by the firm as retained earnings.

   The items deducted will typically include tax expense, financing expense (interest expense), and minority interest. Likewise, preferred stock dividends will be subtracted too, though they are not an expense.

   a. Net income
   b. Generally accepted accounting principles
   c. Long-term liabilities
   d. Matching principle

4. A _____ is a company that owns enough voting stock in another firm to control management and operations by influencing or electing its board of directors; the second company being deemed as a subsidiary of the _____. The definition of a _____ differs from jurisdiction to jurisdiction, with the definition normally being defined by way of laws dealing with companies in that jurisdiction.

   The _____-subsidiary company relationship is defined by Part 1.2, Division 6, Section 46 of the Corporations Act 2001 (Cth), which states:

   A body corporate (in this section called the first body) is a subsidiary of another body corporate if, and only if:

   (a) the other body:

   (i) controls the composition of the first body's board; or

   (ii) is in a position to cast, or control the casting of, more than one-half of the maximum number of votes that might be cast at a general meeting of the first body; or

   (iii) holds more than one-half of the issued share capital of the first body (excluding any part of that issued share capital that carries no right to participate beyond a specified amount in a distribution of either profits or capital); or

   (b) the first body is a subsidiary of a subsidiary of the other body.

34   Chapter 7. Intercompany Inventory Transactions

    a. BMC Software, Inc.   b. 3M Company
    c. Subsidiary   d. Parent company

5. In accounting/accountancy, _____ are journal entries usually made at the end of an accounting period to allocate income and expenditure to the period in which they actually occurred. The revenue recognition principle is the basis of making _____ that pertain to unearned and accrued revenues under accrual-basis accounting. They are sometimes called Balance Day adjustments because they are made on balance day.

    a. Earnings before interest, taxes, depreciation and amortization   b. Adjusting entries
    c. Accrual   d. Accrued expense

6. _____ is a specific term used in companies' financial reporting from the company-whole point of view. Because that use excludes the effects of changing ownership interest, an economic measure of _____ is necessary for financial analysis from the shareholders' point of view

_____ is defined by the Financial Accounting Standards Board, or FASB, as 'the change in equity [net assets] of a business enterprise during a period from transactions and other events and circumstances from nonowner sources. It includes all changes in equity during a period except those resulting from investments by owners and distributions to owners.'

_____ is the sum of net income and other items that must bypass the income statement because they have not been realized, including items like an unrealized holding gain or loss from available for sale securities and foreign currency translation gains or losses.

    a. BNSF Railway   b. BMC Software, Inc.
    c. Comprehensive income   d. 3M Company

7. _____ are financial statements that factor the holding company's subsidiaries into its aggregated accounting figure. It is a representation of how the holding company is doing as a group. The consolidated accounts should provide a true and fair view of the financial and operating conditions of the group.

    a. Redemption value   b. Replacement cost
    c. Committee on Accounting Procedure   d. Consolidated financial statements

8. _____ are formal records of a business' financial activities.

In British English, including United Kingdom company law, _____ are often referred to as accounts, although the term _____ is also used, particularly by accountants.

_____ provide an overview of a business' financial condition in both short and long term.

    a. Statement of retained earnings   b. 3M Company
    c. Notes to the financial statements   d. Financial statements

Chapter 7. Intercompany Inventory Transactions

9. In finance, _____ is the process of estimating the potential market value of a financial asset or liability. They can be done on assets (for example, investments in marketable securities such as stocks, options, business enterprises, or intangible assets such as patents and trademarks) or on liabilities (e.g., Bonds issued by a company.) A _____ is required in many contexts including investment analysis, capital budgeting, merger and acquisition transactions, financial reporting, taxable events to determine the proper tax liability, and in litigation.

   a. Disclosure
   b. Daybook
   c. Valuation
   d. Vyborg Appeal

10. _____ in accounting is the process of treating equity investments, usually 20-50%, in associate companies. The investor keeps such equities as an asset. Proportional share of associate company's net income increases the investment, and proportional payment of dividends decreases it.

    a. ABC Television Network
    b. AIG
    c. Out-of-pocket
    d. Equity method

11. _____ refers to a business or organization attempting to acquire goods or services to accomplish the goals of the enterprise. Though there are several organizations that attempt to set standards in the _____ process, processes can vary greatly between organizations. Typically the word e;_____e; is not used interchangeably with the word e;procuremente;, since procurement typically includes Expediting, Supplier Quality, and Traffic and Logistics (T'L) in addition to _____.

    a. Consignor
    b. Purchasing
    c. Supply chain
    d. Free port

Chapter 8. Intercompany Indebtedness

1. _____ is that which is owed; usually referencing assets owed, but the term can also cover moral obligations and other interactions not requiring money. In the case of assets, _____ is a means of using future purchasing power in the present before a summation has been earned. Some companies and corporations use _____ as a part of their overall corporate finance strategy.

    a. Debt
    b. Debenture
    c. Loan
    d. Lender

2. In finance, a _____ is a debt security, in which the authorized issuer owes the holders a debt and, depending on the terms of the _____, is obliged to pay interest (the coupon) and/or to repay the principal at a later date, termed maturity. It is a formal contract to repay borrowed money with interest at fixed intervals.

    Thus a _____ is like a loan: the issuer is the borrower, the _____ holder is the lender, and the coupon is the interest.

    a. Revenue bonds
    b. Zero-coupon bond
    c. Bond
    d. Coupon rate

3. Discounting is a financial mechanism in which a debtor obtains the right to delay payments to a creditor, for a defined period of time, in exchange for a charge or fee. Essentially, the party that owes money in the present purchases the right to delay the payment until some future date. The _____, or charge, is simply the difference between the original amount owed in the present and the amount that has to be paid in the future to settle the debt.

    a. Risk aversion
    b. Discounting
    c. Discount factor
    d. Discount

4. _____, in finance and accounting, means stated value or face value. From this comes the expressions at par (at the _____), over par (over _____) and under par (under _____).

    _____ is a nominal value of a security which is determined by an issuer company at a minimum price. _____ of an equity (a stock) is a somewhat archaic concept. The _____ of a stock was the share price upon initial offering; the issuing company promised not to issue further shares below _____, so investors could be confident that no one else was receiving a more favorable issue price. This was far more important in unregulated equity markets than in the regulated markets that exist today.

    a. Net worth
    b. Restructuring
    c. Creditor
    d. Par value

5. A _____ is the pinnacle activity involved in selling products or services in return for money or other compensation. It is an act of completion of a commercial activity.

    A _____ is completed by the seller, the owner of the goods.

    a. Tertiary sector of economy
    b. High yield stock
    c. Maturity
    d. Sale

6. A _____ is like a lottery bond issued by the United Kingdom government's National Savings and Investments scheme. The government promises to buy back the bond, on request, for its original price.

Chapter 8. Intercompany Indebtedness

_____s were introduced by the government in 1956, with the aim of encouraging saving and controlling inflation, with the first bonds going on sale on 1 November of that year.

a. Revenue bonds
c. Callable bond
b. Zero-coupon bond
d. Premium Bond

7. In accounting, _____ or carrying value is the value of an asset according to its balance sheet account balance. For assets, the value is based on the original cost of the asset less any depreciation, amortization or impairment costs made against the asset. Traditionally, a company's _____ is its total assets minus intangible assets and liabilities.

a. Book value
c. Depreciation
b. Generally accepted accounting principles
d. Matching principle

8. _____ is equal to the income that a firm has after subtracting costs and expenses from the total revenue. _____ can be distributed among holders of common stock as a dividend or held by the firm as retained earnings.

The items deducted will typically include tax expense, financing expense (interest expense), and minority interest. Likewise, preferred stock dividends will be subtracted too, though they are not an expense.

a. Matching principle
c. Long-term liabilities
b. Generally accepted accounting principles
d. Net income

9. _____ in accounting is the process of treating equity investments, usually 20-50%, in associate companies. The investor keeps such equities as an asset. Proportional share of associate company's net income increases the investment, and proportional payment of dividends decreases it.

a. Out-of-pocket
c. Equity method
b. ABC Television Network
d. AIG

10. In economics, business, retail, and accounting, a _____ is the value of money that has been used up to produce something, and hence is not available for use anymore. In economics, a _____ is an alternative that is given up as a result of a decision. In business, the _____ may be one of acquisition, in which case the amount of money expended to acquire it is counted as _____.

a. Cost allocation
c. Cost of quality
b. Prime cost
d. Cost

Chapter 9. Consolidation Ownership Issues

1. A _____, in business matters, is an entity that is controlled by a bigger and more powerful entity. The controlled entity is called a company, corporation, or limited liability company, and the controlling entity is called its parent (or the parent company.) The reason for this distinction is that a lone company cannot be a _____ of any organization; only an entity representing a legal fiction as a separate entity can be a _____.

   a. 3M Company
   b. Parent company
   c. Subsidiary
   d. BMC Software, Inc.

2. _____ is the state or fact of exclusive rights and control over property, which may be an object, land/real estate or intellectual property. An _____ right is also referred to as title.

   _____ is the key building block in the development of the capitalist socio-economic system.

   a. Administrative proceeding
   b. Encumbrance
   c. Ownership
   d. ABC Television Network

3. _____ is typically a 'higher ranking' stock than voting shares, and its terms are negotiated between the corporation and the investor.

   _____ usually carries no voting rights, but may carry superior priority over common stock in the payment of dividends and upon liquidation. _____ may carry a dividend that is paid out prior to any dividends being paid to common stock holders.

   a. Restricted stock
   b. Preferred stock
   c. Cash flow
   d. Gross income

4. A _____ is a company that owns enough voting stock in another firm to control management and operations by influencing or electing its board of directors; the second company being deemed as a subsidiary of the _____. The definition of a _____ differs from jurisdiction to jurisdiction, with the definition normally being defined by way of laws dealing with companies in that jurisdiction.

   The _____-subsidiary company relationship is defined by Part 1.2, Division 6, Section 46 of the Corporations Act 2001 (Cth), which states:

Chapter 9. Consolidation Ownership Issues

A body corporate (in this section called the first body) is a subsidiary of another body corporate if, and only if:

  (a) the other body:

    (i) controls the composition of the first body's board; or

    (ii) is in a position to cast, or control the casting of, more than one-half of the maximum number of votes that might be cast at a general meeting of the first body; or

    (iii) holds more than one-half of the issued share capital of the first body (excluding any part of that issued share capital that carries no right to participate beyond a specified amount in a distribution of either profits or capital); or

  (b) the first body is a subsidiary of a subsidiary of the other body.

a. 3M Company
b. Subsidiary
c. BMC Software, Inc.
d. Parent company

5. The _____ is the former authoritative body of the American Institute of Certified Public Accountants (AICPA.) It was created by the American Institute of Certified Public Accountants in 1959 and issued pronouncements on accounting principles until 1973, when it was replaced by the Financial Accounting Standards Board (FASB.)

The _____ was disbanded in the hopes that the smaller, fully-independent FASB could more effectively create accounting standards.

a. International Federation of Accountants
b. Institute of Management Accountants
c. American Payroll Association
d. Accounting Principles Board

6. _____ is a form of corporation equity ownership represented in the securities. It is a stock whose dividends are based on market fluctuations. It is dangerous in comparison to preferred shares and some other investment options, in that in the event of bankruptcy, _____ investors receive their funds after preferred stock holders, bondholders, creditors, etc. On the other hand, common shares on average perform better than preferred shares or bonds over time.

a. Common Stock
b. Stock split
c. Growth investing
d. 3M Company

7. _____ in accounting is the process of treating equity investments, usually 20-50%, in associate companies. The investor keeps such equities as an asset. Proportional share of associate company's net income increases the investment, and proportional payment of dividends decreases it.

a. ABC Television Network
b. Out-of-pocket
c. AIG
d. Equity Method

8. A _____ is the pinnacle activity involved in selling products or services in return for money or other compensation. It is an act of completion of a commercial activity.

A _____ is completed by the seller, the owner of the goods.

a. Maturity
c. High yield stock
b. Tertiary sector of economy
d. Sale

9. A _____ or reacquired stock is stock which is bought back by the issuing company, reducing the amount of outstanding stock on the open market ('open market' including insiders' holdings).

Stock repurchases are often used as a tax-efficient method to put cash into shareholders' hands, rather than pay dividends. Sometimes, companies do this when they feel that their stock is undervalued on the open market.

a. Matching principle
c. Treasury stock
b. Cost of goods sold
d. Net profit

10. In accounting/accountancy, _____ are journal entries usually made at the end of an accounting period to allocate income and expenditure to the period in which they actually occurred. The revenue recognition principle is the basis of making _____ that pertain to unearned and accrued revenues under accrual-basis accounting. They are sometimes called Balance Day adjustments because they are made on balance day.

a. Accrual
c. Accrued expense
b. Adjusting entries
d. Earnings before interest, taxes, depreciation and amortization

11. _____ is a specific term used in companies' financial reporting from the company-whole point of view. Because that use excludes the effects of changing ownership interest, an economic measure of _____ is necessary for financial analysis from the shareholders' point of view

_____ is defined by the Financial Accounting Standards Board, or FASB, as 'the change in equity [net assets] of a business enterprise during a period from transactions and other events and circumstances from nonowner sources. It includes all changes in equity during a period except those resulting from investments by owners and distributions to owners.'

_____ is the sum of net income and other items that must bypass the income statement because they have not been realized, including items like an unrealized holding gain or loss from available for sale securities and foreign currency translation gains or losses.

a. BNSF Railway
c. 3M Company
b. BMC Software, Inc.
d. Comprehensive income

12. _____ are payments made by a corporation to its shareholder members. It is the portion of corporate profits paid out to stockholders. When a corporation earns a profit or surplus, that money can be put to two uses: it can either be re-invested in the business (called retained earnings), or it can be paid to the shareholders as a dividend.

a. Dividend yield
c. Dividend payout ratio
b. Dividends
d. Dividend stripping

13. _____ is equal to the income that a firm has after subtracting costs and expenses from the total revenue. _____ can be distributed among holders of common stock as a dividend or held by the firm as retained earnings.

The items deducted will typically include tax expense, financing expense (interest expense), and minority interest. Likewise, preferred stock dividends will be subtracted too, though they are not an expense.

a. Generally accepted accounting principles
b. Net income
c. Matching principle
d. Long-term liabilities

42 Chapter 10. Additional Consolidation Reporting Issues

1. _____ is the balance of the amounts of cash being received and paid by a business during a defined period of time, sometimes tied to a specific project. Measurement of _____ can be used

   - to evaluate the state or performance of a business or project.
   - to determine problems with liquidity. Being profitable does not necessarily mean being liquid. A company can fail because of a shortage of cash, even while profitable.
   - to project rate of returns. The time of _____s into and out of projects are used as inputs to financial models such as internal rate of return, and net present value.
   - to examine income or growth of a business when it is believed that accrual accounting concepts do not represent economic realities. Alternately, _____ can be used to 'validate' the net income generated by accrual accounting.

   _____ as a generic term may be used differently depending on context, and certain _____ definitions may be adapted by analysts and users for their own uses. Common terms include operating _____ and free _____.

   a. Controlling interest
   b. Cash flow
   c. Flow-through entity
   d. Commercial paper

2. In financial accounting, a _____ or Statement of cash flows is a financial statement that shows a company's flow of cash. The money coming into the business is called cash inflow, and money going out from the business is called cash outflow. The statement shows how changes in balance sheet and income accounts affect cash and cash equivalents, and breaks the analysis down to operating, investing, and financing activities.

   a. 3M Company
   b. BMC Software, Inc.
   c. BNSF Railway
   d. Cash flow statement

3. An _____ is the buying of one company by another. An _____ may be friendly or hostile. In the former case, the companies cooperate in negotiations; in the latter case, the takeover target is unwilling to be bought or the target's board has no prior knowledge of the offer. _____ usually refers to a purchase of a smaller firm by a larger one. Sometimes, however, a smaller firm will acquire management control of a larger or longer established company and keep its name for the combined entity. This is known as a reverse takeover.

   a. ABC Television Network
   b. AIG
   c. Acquisition
   d. AMEX

4. _____ were documents issued by the Committee on Accounting Procedure between 1938 and 1959 on various accounting problems. They were discontinued with the dissolution of the Committee in 1959 under a recommendation from the Special Committee on Research Program. In all, 51 bulletins were issued, however, the lack of binding authority over AICPA's membership reduced the influence of, and compliance with the content of the bulletins.

   a. ABC Television Network
   b. Other postemployment benefits
   c. AIG
   d. Accounting Research Bulletins

5. _____ are financial statements that factor the holding company's subsidiaries into its aggregated accounting figure. It is a representation of how the holding company is doing as a group. The consolidated accounts should provide a true and fair view of the financial and operating conditions of the group.

   a. Replacement cost
   b. Committee on Accounting Procedure
   c. Redemption value
   d. Consolidated financial statements

6. _____ are formal records of a business' financial activities.

Chapter 10. Additional Consolidation Reporting Issues

In British English, including United Kingdom company law, _____ are often referred to as accounts, although the term _____ is also used, particularly by accountants.

_____ provide an overview of a business' financial condition in both short and long term.

a. 3M Company
c. Notes to the financial statements

b. Financial Statements
d. Statement of retained earnings

7. A _____ is a company that owns enough voting stock in another firm to control management and operations by influencing or electing its board of directors; the second company being deemed as a subsidiary of the _____. The definition of a _____ differs from jurisdiction to jurisdiction, with the definition normally being defined by way of laws dealing with companies in that jurisdiction.

The _____-subsidiary company relationship is defined by Part 1.2, Division 6, Section 46 of the Corporations Act 2001 (Cth), which states:

A body corporate (in this section called the first body) is a subsidiary of another body corporate if, and only if:

(a) the other body:

(i) controls the composition of the first body's board; or

(ii) is in a position to cast, or control the casting of, more than one-half of the maximum number of votes that might be cast at a general meeting of the first body; or

(iii) holds more than one-half of the issued share capital of the first body (excluding any part of that issued share capital that carries no right to participate beyond a specified amount in a distribution of either profits or capital); or

(b) the first body is a subsidiary of a subsidiary of the other body.

a. Subsidiary
c. 3M Company

b. BMC Software, Inc.
d. Parent company

8. In accounting/accountancy, _____ are journal entries usually made at the end of an accounting period to allocate income and expenditure to the period in which they actually occurred. The revenue recognition principle is the basis of making _____ that pertain to unearned and accrued revenues under accrual-basis accounting. They are sometimes called Balance Day adjustments because they are made on balance day.

a. Accrual
c. Earnings before interest, taxes, depreciation and amortization

b. Adjusting entries
d. Accrued expense

Chapter 10. Additional Consolidation Reporting Issues

9. _____ is a specific term used in companies' financial reporting from the company-whole point of view. Because that use excludes the effects of changing ownership interest, an economic measure of _____ is necessary for financial analysis from the shareholders' point of view

_____ is defined by the Financial Accounting Standards Board, or FASB, as 'the change in equity [net assets] of a business enterprise during a period from transactions and other events and circumstances from nonowner sources. It includes all changes in equity during a period except those resulting from investments by owners and distributions to owners.'

_____ is the sum of net income and other items that must bypass the income statement because they have not been realized, including items like an unrealized holding gain or loss from available for sale securities and foreign currency translation gains or losses.

 a. BMC Software, Inc.
 b. 3M Company
 c. BNSF Railway
 d. Comprehensive income

10. _____ is the state or fact of exclusive rights and control over property, which may be an object, land/real estate or intellectual property. An _____ right is also referred to as title.

_____ is the key building block in the development of the capitalist socio-economic system.

 a. Ownership
 b. ABC Television Network
 c. Administrative proceeding
 d. Encumbrance

11. A _____, in business matters, is an entity that is controlled by a bigger and more powerful entity. The controlled entity is called a company, corporation, or limited liability company, and the controlling entity is called its parent (or the parent company.) The reason for this distinction is that a lone company cannot be a _____ of any organization; only an entity representing a legal fiction as a separate entity can be a _____.
 a. 3M Company
 b. Parent company
 c. BMC Software, Inc.
 d. Subsidiary

12. In accounting, _____ has a very specific meaning. It is an outflow of cash or other valuable assets from a person or company to another person or company. This outflow of cash is generally one side of a trade for products or services that have equal or better current or future value to the buyer than to the seller.
 a. AIG
 b. ABC Television Network
 c. Expense
 d. AMEX

13. An _____ is a tax levied on the financial income of people, corporations, or other legal entities. Various _____ systems exist, with varying degrees of tax incidence. Income taxation can be progressive, proportional, or regressive.
 a. Individual Retirement Arrangement
 b. Ordinary income
 c. Implied level of government service
 d. Income tax

Chapter 10. Additional Consolidation Reporting Issues

14. At its simplest, a company's _____ as it sometimes called, is computed in by multiplying the income before tax number, as reported to shareholders, by the appropriate tax rate. In reality, the computation is typically considerably more complex due to things such as expenses considered not deductible by taxing authorities ('add backs'), the range of tax rates applicable to various levels of income, different tax rates in different jurisdictions, multiple layers of tax on income, and other issues.

Historically, in many places, a revenue-expense method was used, in which the income statement was seen as primary, and the balance sheet as secondary.

a. 3M Company
c. Total Expense Ratio
b. Payroll
d. Tax expense

15. _____ is generally understood in financial circles as the point at which revenue is recognized, typically through a transaction which involves the exchange of an asset, product, or service for cash or its equivalents.

This approach gives the accounting division a strictly objective basis for changing the books. For example, a homeowner may believe that his house has grown in value during a strong market, or fallen in value during a weak market, but until the house is actually sold for a specific price to a specific buyer, the change in value can only be estimated and is considered unrealized.

a. Valuation
c. Merck ' Co., Inc.
b. Total-factor productivity
d. Realization

16. _____, in accrual accounting, is any account where the asset or liability is not realized until a future date (accounting period), e.g. annuities, charges, taxes, income, etc. The _____ item may be carried, dependent on type of deferral, as either an asset or liability.

a. Payroll
c. Cash basis accounting
b. Pro forma
d. Deferred

17. _____, in accrual accounting, (e.g. advance payment received from a client) is, according to revenue recognition, revenue not earned until the delivery of goods or services, which until then, is still owed to the payer, hence remaining a liability.

_____, sometimes referred to as deferred revenue or unearned revenue, shares characteristics with accrued expense with the difference that a liability to be covered latter is cash received FROM a counterpart, while goods or services are to be delivered in a latter period, when such income item is earned, the related revenue item is recognized, and the same amount is deducted from deferred revenues.

a. Deferred income
c. Matching principle
b. Treasury stock
d. Gross sales

18. _____ are the earnings returned on the initial investment amount.

In the US, the Financial Accounting Standards Board (FASB) requires companies' income statements to report _____ for each of the major categories of the income statement: continuing operations, discontinued operations, extraordinary items, and net income.

The _____ formula does not include preferred dividends for categories outside of continued operations and net income.

a. Invested capital
b. Earnings per share
c. Earnings yield
d. Average accounting return

Chapter 11. Multinational Accounting

1. The _____ (IMF) is an international organization that oversees the global financial system by following the macroeconomic policies of its member countries, in particular those with an impact on exchange rates and the balance of payments. It is an organization formed to stabilize international exchange rates and facilitate development. It also offers financial and technical assistance to its members, making it an international lender of last resort.
   a. ABC Television Network
   b. International Monetary Fund
   c. AIG
   d. IMF

2. The _____ is an international organization that oversees the global financial system by following the macroeconomic policies of its member countries, in particular those with an impact on exchange rates and the balance of payments. It is an organization formed to stabilize international exchange rates and facilitate development. It also offers financial and technical assistance to its members, making it an international lender of last resort.
   a. AIG
   b. ABC Television Network
   c. IMF
   d. International Monetary Fund

3. The _____ or East Asia Economic Group (EAEG) is a regional free trade zone (FTA) proposed in 1990 by former Malaysian Prime Minister Dr. Mahathir bin Mohamad and encompasses the Association of Southeast Asian Nations member states, China, South Korea and Japan. Japan though refused participation out of its loyalty to the US.

   The _____ was a reaction to ASEAN's integration into the Asia-Pacific Economic Cooperation (APEC) by Dr. Mahathir, who is known for his strong Asian standpoint.

   a. Institute of Management Accountants
   b. American Payroll Association
   c. Australian Accounting Standards Board
   d. East Asia Economic Caucus

4. The International Organization for Standardization (Organisation internationale de normalisation), widely known as _____ , is an international-standard-setting body composed of representatives from various national standards organizations. Founded on 23 February 1947, the organization promulgates worldwide proprietary industrial and commercial standards. It is headquartered in Geneva, Switzerland.
   a. AIG
   b. AMEX
   c. ABC Television Network
   d. ISO

5. The _____, widely known as ISO , is an international-standard-setting body composed of representatives from various national standards organizations. Founded on 23 February 1947, the organization promulgates worldwide proprietary industrial and commercial standards. It is headquartered in Geneva, Switzerland.
   a. AMEX
   b. International Organization for Standardization
   c. ABC Television Network
   d. AIG

6. The _____ is a trilateral trade bloc in North America created by the governments of the United States, Canada, and Mexico. The agreement creating the trade bloc came into force on January 1, 1994. It superseded the Canada-United States Free Trade Agreement between the U.S. and Canada.
   a. Collusion
   b. Chief executive officer
   c. Moving average
   d. North American Free Trade Agreement

7. In monetary economics _____ can refer either to a particular _____, for example British Pounds or United States Dollars, or, to the coins and banknotes of a particular _____, which actually form only a small part of the monetary base of a nation's money supply. The other part of a nation's money supply consists of money deposited in banks (sometimes called deposit money), ownership of which can be transferred by means of checks (cheques in the United Kingdom and Australia) or other forms of money transfer such as credit and debit cards. Deposit money and _____ are 'money' in the sense that both are acceptable as a means of exchange, but money need not necessarily be '_____'.

   a. Currency
   b. BMC Software, Inc.
   c. BNSF Railway
   d. 3M Company

8. The _____ is a private, not-for-profit organization whose primary purpose is to develop generally accepted accounting principles (GAAP) within the United States in the public's interest. The Securities and Exchange Commission (SEC) designated the _____ as the organization responsible for setting accounting standards for public companies in the U.S. It was created in 1973, replacing the Accounting Principles Board and the Committee on Accounting Procedure of the American Institute of Certified Public Accountants. The _____'s mission is 'to establish and improve standards of financial accounting and reporting for the guidance and education of the public, including issuers, auditors, and users of financial information.'

   The _____ is not a governmental body.

   a. Governmental Accounting Standards Board
   b. Public company
   c. Fannie Mae
   d. Financial Accounting Standards Board

9. _____, commonly known as FAS 133, is an accounting standard issued in January 2001 by the Financial Accounting Standards Board (FASB) that provides companies with the ability to measure all assets and liabilities on their balance sheet at e;fair valuee;. This standard was created in response to significant hedging losses involving derivatives years ago and the attempt to control and manage corporate hedging as risk management not earnings management.

   a. Statements of Financial Accounting Standards No. 133, Accounting for Derivative Instruments and Hedging Activities
   b. Factor
   c. Welfare
   d. Maturity

10. In finance, the _____ between two currencies specifies how much one currency is worth in terms of the other. It is the value of a foreign nation's currency in terms of the home nation's currency. For example an _____ of 102 Japanese yen to the United States dollar means that JPY 102 is worth the same as USD 1.

    a. AIG
    b. Exchange rate
    c. ABC Television Network
    d. AMEX

11. In economics, a _____, in its common usage, is a currency not backed by a national government (and not necessarily legal tender), and intended to trade only in a small area. These currencies are also referred to as community currency, or complementary currency. They encompass a wide range of forms, both physically and financially, and often are associated with a particular economic discourse.

    a. BMC Software, Inc.
    b. 3M Company
    c. BNSF Railway
    d. Local currency

12. In foreign exchange markets, the _____ is the first currency in a currency pair. The second currency is named the quote currency (counter currency, terms currency.) Exchange rates are quoted in per unit of the _____.

Chapter 11. Multinational Accounting

a. BMC Software, Inc.
b. BNSF Railway
c. 3M Company
d. Base currency

13. The spot price or _____ of a commodity, a security or a currency is the price that is quoted for immediate (spot) settlement (payment and delivery.) Spot settlement is normally one or two business days from trade date. This is in contrast with the forward price established in a forward contract or futures contract, where contract terms (price) are set now, but delivery and payment will occur at a future date.

a. Financial instruments
b. Market price
c. Market liquidity
d. Spot rate

14. _____ is the monetary unit of account of the principal economic environment in which an economic entity operates.

Statement of Financial Standards No. 52 (SFAS 52) is the primary source of GAAP for translation of foreign currency financial statements.

a. BNSF Railway
b. BMC Software, Inc.
c. Functional currency
d. 3M Company

15. _____s are cash, evidence of an ownership interest in an entity or deliver, cash or another _____.

_____s can be categorized by form depending on whether they are cash instruments or derivative instruments:

- Cash instruments are _____s whose value is determined directly by markets. They can be divided into securities, which are readily transferable, and other cash instruments such as loans and deposits, where both borrower and lender have to agree on a transfer.
- Derivative instruments are _____s which derive their value from the value and characteristics of one or more underlying assets. They can be divided into exchange-traded derivatives and over-the-counter (OTC) derivatives.

Alternatively, _____s can be categorized by 'asset class' depending on whether they are equity based (reflecting ownership of the issuing entity) or debt based (reflecting a loan the investor has made to the issuing entity.) If it is debt, it can be further categorised into short term (less than one year) or long term.

Foreign Exchange instruments and transactions are neither debt nor equity based and belong in their own category.

a. Financial instruments
b. Mark-to-market
c. Financial instrument
d. Market price

16. _____ are cash, evidence of an ownership interest in an entity, or a contractual right to receive, or deliver, cash or another financial instrument.

Chapter 11. Multinational Accounting

_____ can be categorized by form depending on whether they are cash instruments or derivative instruments:

- Cash instruments are _____ whose value is determined directly by markets. They can be divided into securities, which are readily transferable, and other cash instruments such as loans and deposits, where both borrower and lender have to agree on a transfer.
- Derivative instruments are _____ which derive their value from the value and characteristics of one or more underlying assets. They can be divided into exchange-traded derivatives and over-the-counter (OTC) derivatives.

Alternatively, _____ can be categorized by 'asset class' depending on whether they are equity based (reflecting ownership of the issuing entity) or debt based (reflecting a loan the investor has made to the issuing entity.) If it is debt, it can be further categorised into short term (less than one year) or long term.

Foreign Exchange instruments and transactions are neither debt nor equity based and belong in their own category.

a. Market liquidity
b. Spot rate
c. Transfer agent
d. Financial instruments

17. The _____ is a daily reference rate based on the interest rates at which banks borrow unsecured funds from other banks in the London wholesale money market. It is roughly comparable to the U.S. Federal funds rate.

During 1984 it became apparent that an increasing number of banks were trading actively in a variety of relatively new market instruments, notably interest rate swaps, foreign currency options and forward rate agreements.

a. BNSF Railway
b. BMC Software, Inc.
c. 3M Company
d. London Interbank Offered Rate

18. _____ is the balance of the amounts of cash being received and paid by a business during a defined period of time, sometimes tied to a specific project. Measurement of _____ can be used

- to evaluate the state or performance of a business or project.
- to determine problems with liquidity. Being profitable does not necessarily mean being liquid. A company can fail because of a shortage of cash, even while profitable.
- to project rate of returns. The time of _____s into and out of projects are used as inputs to financial models such as internal rate of return, and net present value.
- to examine income or growth of a business when it is believed that accrual accounting concepts do not represent economic realities. Alternately, _____ can be used to 'validate' the net income generated by accrual accounting.

_____ as a generic term may be used differently depending on context, and certain _____ definitions may be adapted by analysts and users for their own uses. Common terms include operating _____ and free _____.

Chapter 11. Multinational Accounting

a. Commercial paper
b. Flow-through entity
c. Controlling interest
d. Cash flow

19. A _____ is a hedge of the exposure to the variability of cash flow that

   1. is attributable to a particular risk associated with a recognized asset or liability. Such as all or some future interest payments on variable rate debt or a highly probable forecast transaction and
   2. could affect profit or loss

   a. 3M Company
   b. Credit risk
   c. Currency risk
   d. Cash flow hedge

20. Discounting is a financial mechanism in which a debtor obtains the right to delay payments to a creditor, for a defined period of time, in exchange for a charge or fee. Essentially, the party that owes money in the present purchases the right to delay the payment until some future date. The _____, or charge, is simply the difference between the original amount owed in the present and the amount that has to be paid in the future to settle the debt.

   a. Discount
   b. Risk aversion
   c. Discount factor
   d. Discounting

21. In finance, a _____ is a debt security, in which the authorized issuer owes the holders a debt and, depending on the terms of the _____, is obliged to pay interest (the coupon) and/or to repay the principal at a later date, termed maturity. It is a formal contract to repay borrowed money with interest at fixed intervals.

   Thus a _____ is like a loan: the issuer is the borrower, the _____ holder is the lender, and the coupon is the interest.

   a. Coupon rate
   b. Zero-coupon bond
   c. Revenue bonds
   d. Bond

22. A _____ is the pinnacle activity involved in selling products or services in return for money or other compensation. It is an act of completion of a commercial activity.

   A _____ is completed by the seller, the owner of the goods.

   a. Tertiary sector of economy
   b. Sale
   c. High yield stock
   d. Maturity

23. In business and accounting, _____ are everything of value that is owned by a person or company. It is a claim on the property your income of a borrower. The balance sheet of a firm records the monetary value of the _____ owned by the firm.

   a. Accrual basis accounting
   b. Earnings before interest, taxes, depreciation and amortization
   c. Accounts receivable
   d. Assets

Chapter 11. Multinational Accounting

24. In financial accounting, a _____ is defined as an obligation of an entity arising from past transactions or events, the settlement of which may result in the transfer or use of assets, provision of services or other yielding of economic benefits in the future.

   a. Vested
   b. False Claims Act
   c. Corporate governance
   d. Liability

25. A _____ is any one of a variety of different systems, institutions, procedures, social relations and infrastructures whereby persons trade, and goods and services are exchanged, forming part of the economy. It is an arrangement that allows buyers and sellers to exchange things. _____s vary in size, range, geographic scale, location, types and variety of human communities, as well as the types of goods and services traded.

   a. Perfect competition
   b. Market Failure
   c. Recession
   d. Market

26. An _____ is a tax levied on the financial income of people, corporations, or other legal entities. Various _____ systems exist, with varying degrees of tax incidence. Income taxation can be progressive, proportional, or regressive.

   a. Ordinary income
   b. Implied level of government service
   c. Income Tax
   d. Individual Retirement Arrangement

27. _____, also called fair price (in a commonplace conflation of the two distinct concepts), is a concept used in finance and economics, defined as a rational and unbiased estimate of the potential market price of a good, service, or asset, taking into account such objective factors as:

   - acquisition/production/distribution costs, replacement costs, or costs of close substitutes
   - actual utility at a given level of development of social productive capability
   - supply vs. demand

   and subjective factors such as

   - risk characteristics
   - cost of capital
   - individually perceived utility

   In accounting, _____ is used as an estimate of the market value of an asset (or liability) for which a market price cannot be determined (usually because there is no established market for the asset.) Under GAAP (FAS 157), _____ is the amount at which the asset could be bought or sold in a current transaction between willing parties, or transferred to an equivalent party, other than in a liquidation sale. This is used for assets whose carrying value is based on mark-to-market valuations; for assets carried at historical cost, the _____ of the asset is not used. One example of where _____ is an issue is a College kitchen with a cost of $2 million which was built 5 years ago.

   a. BMC Software, Inc.
   b. Fair value
   c. BNSF Railway
   d. 3M Company

Chapter 11. Multinational Accounting

28. Simply put, _____ is the value of money figuring in a given amount of interest for a given amount of time. For example 100 dollars of todays money held for a year at 5 percent interest is worth 105 dollars, therefore 100 dollars paid now or 105 dollars paid exactly one year from now is the same amount of payment of money with that given intersest at that given amount of time. This notion dates at least to Martín de Azpilcueta of the School of Salamanca.

a. Time value of money
b. Merck ' Co., Inc.
c. Competition law
d. Collusion

29. _____ is the risk of loss due to a debtor's non-payment of a loan or other line of credit (either the principal or interest (coupon) or both)

Most lenders employ their own models (credit scorecards) to rank potential and existing customers according to risk, and then apply appropriate strategies. With products such as unsecured personal loans or mortgages, lenders charge a higher price for higher risk customers and vice versa. With revolving products such as credit cards and overdrafts, risk is controlled through the setting of credit limits.

a. Market risk
b. Currency risk
c. 3M Company
d. Credit risk

30. _____ means the giving out of information, either voluntarily or to be in compliance with legal regulations or workplace rules.

- In Computer security, full _____ means disclosing full information about vulnerabilities.
- In computing, _____ widget
- Journalism, full _____ refers to disclosing the interests of the writer which may bear on the subject being written about, for example, if the writer has worked with an interview subject in the past.

- In law:
  - The law of England and Wales, _____ refers to a process that may form part of legal proceedings, whereby parties inform to other parties the existence of any relevant documents that are, or have been, in their control. This compares with the process known as discovery in the course of legal proceedings in the United States.
  - In U.S. civil procedure (litigation rules for civil cases), _____ is a stage prior to trial. In civil cases, each party must disclose to the opposing party the following: names of witnesses which it may use to support its side, copies of documents (or mere description of these documents) in its control which it may use to support its side, computation of damages claimed, and certain insurance information. _____ is related to, but technically prior to, the discovery stage.
  - In Company law (known as 'corporate law' in the United States), _____ refers to giving out information about public or limited companies or their officers, which might be kept secret if the company was a private company or a partnership.

- In real property transactions, _____ refers to providing to a buyer information known to the seller or broker/agent concerning the condition or other aspects of real property that would affect the property's value or desirability. These rules regarding what information must be disclosed, and whether the information must be disclosed even if a buyer does not ask, vary from one jurisdiction to the next.

Chapter 11. Multinational Accounting

a. Tax harmonisation
b. Controlled Foreign Corporations
c. Trailing
d. Disclosure

31. _____ is the risk that the value of an investment will decrease due to moves in market factors. The four standard _____ factors are:

- Equity risk, the risk that stock prices will change.
- Interest rate risk, the risk that interest rates will change.
- Currency risk, the risk that foreign exchange rates will change.
- Commodity risk, the risk that commodity prices (e.g. grains, metals) will change.

As with other forms of risk, _____ may be measured in a number of ways. Traditionally, this is done using a Value at Risk methodology. Value at risk is well established as a risk management technique, but it contains a number of limiting assumptions that constrain its accuracy.

a. Currency risk
b. 3M Company
c. Market risk
d. Credit risk

32. _____ is a concept that denotes the precise probability of specific eventualities. Technically, the notion of _____ is independent from the notion of value and, as such, eventualities may have both beneficial and adverse consequences. However, in general usage the convention is to focus only on potential negative impact to some characteristic of value that may arise from a future event.

a. Discount factor
b. Risk adjusted return on capital
c. Discounting
d. Risk

33. The _____ , established in 1848, is the world's oldest futures and options exchange. More than 50 different options and futures contracts are traded by over 3,600 _____ members through open outcry and eTrading. Volumes at the exchange in 2003 were a record breaking 454 million contracts.

a. BMC Software, Inc.
b. 3M Company
c. BNSF Railway
d. Chicago Board of Trade

34. The _____ (often called 'the Chicago Merc,' or 'the Merc') is an American financial and commodity derivative exchange based in Chicago. The _____ was founded in 1898 as the Chicago Butter and Egg Board. Originally, the exchange was a non-profit organization.

a. 3M Company
b. Financial Crimes Enforcement Network
c. Public Company Accounting Oversight Board
d. Chicago Mercantile Exchange

35. NYSE Amex Equities, formerly known as the _____ is an _____ situated in New York. AMEX was a mutual organization, owned by its members. Until 1953 it was known as the New York Curb Exchange.

a. American Stock Exchange
b. AMEX
c. AIG
d. ABC Television Network

36. The _____ (CBOE), located at 400 South LaSalle Street in Chicago, is the largest U.S. options exchange with annual trading volume that hovered around one billion contracts at the end of 2007. _____ offers options on over 2,200 companies, 22 stock indexes, and 140 exchange-traded funds (ETFs.)

Chapter 11. Multinational Accounting

The exchange, regulated by the Securities and Exchange Commission, was established in 1973.

a. CBOE
b. BMC Software, Inc.
c. 3M Company
d. Chicago Board Options Exchange

37. The _____ , located at 400 South LaSalle Street in Chicago, is the largest U.S. options exchange with annual trading volume that hovered around one billion contracts at the end of 2007. _____ offers options on over 2,200 companies, 22 stock indexes, and 140 exchange-traded funds (ETFs.)

The exchange, regulated by the Securities and Exchange Commission, was established in 1973.

a. 3M Company
b. BMC Software, Inc.
c. Pacific Exchange
d. Chicago Board Options Exchange

38. In finance, an _____ is a contract between a buyer and a seller that gives the buyer the right--but not the obligation--to buy or to sell a particular asset (the underlying asset) at a later time at an agreed price. In return for granting the _____, the seller collects a payment (the premium) from the buyer. A call _____ gives the buyer the right to buy the underlying asset; a put _____ gives the buyer of the _____ the right to sell the underlying asset.

a. ABC Television Network
b. AMEX
c. AIG
d. Option

39. The _____ was a regional stock exchange with a main exchange floor and building in San Francisco, California, USA and a branch in Los Angeles, California, USA. Its history began with the founding of the San Francisco Stock and Bond Exchange in 1882 and the Los Angeles Oil Exchange in 1889. In 1957, the two exchanges merged to create the Pacific Coast Stock Exchange, though trading floors were maintained in both cities.

a. BMC Software, Inc.
b. 3M Company
c. Chicago Board Options Exchange
d. Pacific Exchange

40. A _____, (formerly a securities exchange) is a corporation or mutual organization which provides 'trading' facilities for stock brokers and traders, to trade stocks and other securities. _____s also provide facilities for the issue and redemption of securities as well as other financial instruments and capital events including the payment of income and dividends. The securities traded on a _____ include: shares issued by companies, unit trusts, derivatives, pooled investment products and bonds.

a. BMC Software, Inc.
b. BNSF Railway
c. 3M Company
d. Stock Exchange

41. In options, the _____ is a key variable in a derivatives contract between two parties. Where the contract requires delivery of the underlying instrument, the trade will be at the _____, regardless of the spot price (market price) of the underlying instrument at that time.

Definition - The fixed price at which the owner of an option can purchase, in the case of a call in the case of a put, the underlying security or commodity.

a. 3M Company
b. Strike price
c. Put option
d. BMC Software, Inc.

42. _____ in economics and business is the result of an exchange and from that trade we assign a numerical monetary value to a good, service or asset. If Alice trades Bob 4 apples for an orange, the _____ of an orange is 4 apples. Inversely, the _____ of an apple is 1/4 oranges.
   a. Price discrimination
   b. Transactional Net Margin Method
   c. Discounts and allowances
   d. Price

43. In finance, a _____ is a derivative in which two counterparties agree to exchange one stream of cash flow against another stream. These streams are called the legs of the _____.

The cash flows are calculated over a notional principal amount, which is usually not exchanged between counterparties.

   a. Total-factor productivity
   b. Department of the Treasury
   c. Controlled Foreign Corporations
   d. Swap

44. _____ refers to a business or organization attempting to acquire goods or services to accomplish the goals of the enterprise. Though there are several organizations that attempt to set standards in the _____ process, processes can vary greatly between organizations. Typically the word e;_____e; is not used interchangeably with the word e;procuremente;, since procurement typically includes Expediting, Supplier Quality, and Traffic and Logistics (T'L) in addition to _____.
   a. Supply chain
   b. Purchasing
   c. Consignor
   d. Free port

45. A _____ is a fungible, negotiable instrument representing financial value. they are broadly categorized into debt securities (such as banknotes, bonds and debentures), and equity securities; e.g., common stocks. The company or other entity issuing the _____ is called the issuer.
   a. Tracking stock
   b. 3M Company
   c. BMC Software, Inc.
   d. Security

46. An _____ is the buying of one company by another. An _____ may be friendly or hostile. In the former case, the companies cooperate in negotiations; in the latter case, the takeover target is unwilling to be bought or the target's board has no prior knowledge of the offer. _____ usually refers to a purchase of a smaller firm by a larger one. Sometimes, however, a smaller firm will acquire management control of a larger or longer established company and keep its name for the combined entity. This is known as a reverse takeover.
   a. Acquisition
   b. AMEX
   c. ABC Television Network
   d. AIG

47. _____ is that which is owed; usually referencing assets owed, but the term can also cover moral obligations and other interactions not requiring money. In the case of assets, _____ is a means of using future purchasing power in the present before a summation has been earned. Some companies and corporations use _____ as a part of their overall corporate finance strategy.

a. Debenture
b. Loan
c. Lender
d. Debt

Chapter 12. Multinational Accounting: Translation of Foreign Entity Statements

1. An American Depository Receipt (or _____) represents the ownership in the shares of a foreign company trading on US financial markets. The stock of many non-US companies trades on US exchanges through the use of _____s. American Depository Receiptss enable US investors to buy shares in foreign companies without undertaking cross-border transactions.
   a. AMEX
   b. ABC Television Network
   c. AIG
   d. American Depository Receipts

2. The _____ of 1977 (15 U.S.C. §§ 78dd-1, et seq.) is a United States federal law known primarily for two of its main provisions, one that addresses accounting transparency requirements under the Securities Exchange Act of 1934 and another concerning bribery of foreign officials.
   a. Foreign Corrupt Practices Act
   b. Pre-emption right
   c. Competition law
   d. Lease

3. _____ is the term used to refer to the standard framework of guidelines for financial accounting used in any given jurisdiction. _____ includes the standards, conventions, and rules accountants follow in recording and summarizing transactions, and in the preparation of financial statements.

   Financial accounting information must be assembled and reported objectively.

   a. Long-term liabilities
   b. Current asset
   c. General ledger
   d. Generally accepted accounting principles

4. _____ are standards and interpretations adopted by the International Accounting Standards Board (IASB.)

   Many of the standards forming part of _____ are known by the older name of International Accounting Standards (IAS.) IAS were issued between 1973 and 2001 by the board of the International Accounting Standards Committee (IASC.)

   a. International Financial Reporting Standards
   b. Out-of-pocket
   c. AIG
   d. ABC Television Network

5. The _____ founded on April 1, 2001 is the successor of the International Accounting Standards Committee (IASC) founded in June 1973 in London. It is responsible for developing the International Financial Reporting Standards (new name for the International Accounting Standards issued after 2001), and promoting the use and application of these standards.

   The _____ is an independent, privately-funded accounting standard-setter based in London, UK.

   a. International Accounting Standards Board
   b. Information Systems Audit and Control Association
   c. Emerging technologies
   d. Institute of Management Accountants

6. _____ was an American financier, banker and art collector who dominated corporate finance and industrial consolidation during his time. In 1892 Morgan arranged the merger of Edison General Electric and Thompson-Houston Electric Company to form General Electric. After financing the creation of the Federal Steel Company he merged the Carnegie Steel Company and several other steel and iron businesses to form the United States Steel Corporation in 1901.
   a. Abby Joseph Cohen
   b. Alan Greenspan
   c. Arthur Betz Laffer
   d. John Pierpont Morgan

Chapter 12. Multinational Accounting: Translation of Foreign Entity Statements 59

7. In monetary economics _____ can refer either to a particular _____, for example British Pounds or United States Dollars, or, to the coins and banknotes of a particular _____, which actually form only a small part of the monetary base of a nation's money supply. The other part of a nation's money supply consists of money deposited in banks (sometimes called deposit money), ownership of which can be transferred by means of checks (cheques in the United Kingdom and Australia) or other forms of money transfer such as credit and debit cards. Deposit money and _____ are 'money' in the sense that both are acceptable as a means of exchange, but money need not necessarily be '_____'.

a. 3M Company
b. Currency
c. BNSF Railway
d. BMC Software, Inc.

8. The _____ is a private, not-for-profit organization whose primary purpose is to develop generally accepted accounting principles (GAAP) within the United States in the public's interest. The Securities and Exchange Commission (SEC) designated the _____ as the organization responsible for setting accounting standards for public companies in the U.S. It was created in 1973, replacing the Accounting Principles Board and the Committee on Accounting Procedure of the American Institute of Certified Public Accountants. The _____'s mission is 'to establish and improve standards of financial accounting and reporting for the guidance and education of the public, including issuers, auditors, and users of financial information.'

The _____ is not a governmental body.

a. Public company
b. Fannie Mae
c. Financial Accounting Standards Board
d. Governmental Accounting Standards Board

9. _____ is the monetary unit of account of the principal economic environment in which an economic entity operates.

Statement of Financial Standards No. 52 (SFAS 52) is the primary source of GAAP for translation of foreign currency financial statements.

a. BMC Software, Inc.
b. 3M Company
c. BNSF Railway
d. Functional currency

10. _____ is a subsection in equity where 'other comprehensive income' is accumulated (summed or 'aggregated'.)

The balance of _____ is presented in the Equity section of the Balance Sheet as is the Retained Earnings balance, which aggregates past and current Earnings, and past and current Dividends.

Other comprehensive income is the difference between net income and comprehensive income and represents the certain gains and losses of the enterprise.

a. Inventory turnover ratio
b. Operating budget
c. Authorised capital
d. Accumulated other comprehensive income

11. _____ is a specific term used in companies' financial reporting from the company-whole point of view. Because that use excludes the effects of changing ownership interest, an economic measure of _____ is necessary for financial analysis from the shareholders' point of view

Chapter 12. Multinational Accounting: Translation of Foreign Entity Statements

_____ is defined by the Financial Accounting Standards Board, or FASB, as 'the change in equity [net assets] of a business enterprise during a period from transactions and other events and circumstances from nonowner sources. It includes all changes in equity during a period except those resulting from investments by owners and distributions to owners.'

_____ is the sum of net income and other items that must bypass the income statement because they have not been realized, including items like an unrealized holding gain or loss from available for sale securities and foreign currency translation gains or losses.

a. BMC Software, Inc.
b. Comprehensive Income
c. BNSF Railway
d. 3M Company

12. _____ is a fee paid on borrowed assets. It is the price paid for the use of borrowed money, or, money earned by deposited funds. Assets that are sometimes lent with _____ include money, shares, consumer goods through hire purchase, major assets such as aircraft, and even entire factories in finance lease arrangements. The _____ is calculated upon the value of the assets in the same manner as upon money.

a. Interest
b. Insolvency
c. AIG
d. ABC Television Network

13. A _____, in business matters, is an entity that is controlled by a bigger and more powerful entity. The controlled entity is called a company, corporation, or limited liability company, and the controlling entity is called its parent (or the parent company.) The reason for this distinction is that a lone company cannot be a _____ of any organization; only an entity representing a legal fiction as a separate entity can be a _____.

a. BMC Software, Inc.
b. Parent company
c. 3M Company
d. Subsidiary

14. _____ are formal records of a business' financial activities.

In British English, including United Kingdom company law, _____ are often referred to as accounts, although the term _____ is also used, particularly by accountants.

_____ provide an overview of a business' financial condition in both short and long term.

a. Statement of retained earnings
b. Financial statements
c. Notes to the financial statements
d. 3M Company

15. _____, commonly known as FAS 133, is an accounting standard issued in January 2001 by the Financial Accounting Standards Board (FASB) that provides companies with the ability to measure all assets and liabilities on their balance sheet at e;fair valuee;. This standard was created in response to significant hedging losses involving derivatives years ago and the attempt to control and manage corporate hedging as risk management not earnings management.

a. Statements of Financial Accounting Standards No. 133, Accounting for Derivative Instruments and Hedging Activities
b. Maturity
c. Welfare
d. Factor

Chapter 12. Multinational Accounting: Translation of Foreign Entity Statements 61

16. A _____ is the pinnacle activity involved in selling products or services in return for money or other compensation. It is an act of completion of a commercial activity.

A _____ is completed by the seller, the owner of the goods.

a. High yield stock
c. Tertiary sector of economy
b. Sale
d. Maturity

17. In law, _____ refers to the process by which a company (or part of a company) is brought to an end, and the assets and property of the company redistributed. _____ can also be referred to as winding-up or dissolution, although dissolution technically refers to the last stage of _____. The process of _____ also arises when customs, an authority or agency in a country responsible for collecting and safeguarding customs duties, determines the final computation or ascertainment of the duties or drawback accruing on an entry.

a. 3M Company
c. BMC Software, Inc.
b. Bankruptcy protection
d. Liquidation

18. _____ means the giving out of information, either voluntarily or to be in compliance with legal regulations or workplace rules.

- In Computer security, full _____ means disclosing full information about vulnerabilities.
- In computing, _____ widget
- Journalism, full _____ refers to disclosing the interests of the writer which may bear on the subject being written about, for example, if the writer has worked with an interview subject in the past.

- In law:
    - The law of England and Wales, _____ refers to a process that may form part of legal proceedings, whereby parties inform to other parties the existence of any relevant documents that are, or have been, in their control. This compares with the process known as discovery in the course of legal proceedings in the United States.
    - In U.S. civil procedure (litigation rules for civil cases), _____ is a stage prior to trial. In civil cases, each party must disclose to the opposing party the following: names of witnesses which it may use to support its side, copies of documents (or mere description of these documents) in its control which it may use to support its side, computation of damages claimed, and certain insurance information. _____ is related to, but technically prior to, the discovery stage.
    - In Company law (known as 'corporate law' in the United States), _____ refers to giving out information about public or limited companies or their officers, which might be kept secret if the company was a private company or a partnership.

- In real property transactions, _____ refers to providing to a buyer information known to the seller or broker/agent concerning the condition or other aspects of real property that would affect the property's value or desirability. These rules regarding what information must be disclosed, and whether the information must be disclosed even if a buyer does not ask, vary from one jurisdiction to the next.

a. Controlled Foreign Corporations
c. Trailing
b. Tax harmonisation
d. Disclosure

Chapter 12. Multinational Accounting: Translation of Foreign Entity Statements

19. Most patent law systems require that a patent application disclose a claimed invention in sufficient detail for the notional person skilled in the art to carry out that claimed invention. This requirement is often known as sufficiency of disclosure or enablement, depending on the jurisdiction.

The _____ lies at the heart and origin of patent law. A state or government grants an inventor, or the inventor's assignee, a monopoly for a given period of time in exchange for the inventor disclosing to the public how to make or practice his or her invention. If a patent fails to contain such information, then the bargain is violated, and the patent is unenforceable.

- a. False Claims Act
- b. Disclosure requirement
- c. Tax patent
- d. Pre-emption right

20. A _____ is a piece of paper, often preprinted in a way designed to help organize material for learning or clear understanding. Students in a school may have 'fill-in-the-blank' sheets of questions, diagrams or maps to help them with their exercises. Students will often use _____s to review what has been taught in class.
- a. 3M Company
- b. BMC Software, Inc.
- c. Value based pricing
- d. Worksheet

21. _____ is the balance of the amounts of cash being received and paid by a business during a defined period of time, sometimes tied to a specific project. Measurement of _____ can be used

- to evaluate the state or performance of a business or project.
- to determine problems with liquidity. Being profitable does not necessarily mean being liquid. A company can fail because of a shortage of cash, even while profitable.
- to project rate of returns. The time of _____s into and out of projects are used as inputs to financial models such as internal rate of return, and net present value.
- to examine income or growth of a business when it is believed that accrual accounting concepts do not represent economic realities. Alternately, _____ can be used to 'validate' the net income generated by accrual accounting.

_____ as a generic term may be used differently depending on context, and certain _____ definitions may be adapted by analysts and users for their own uses. Common terms include operating _____ and free _____.

- a. Controlling interest
- b. Cash flow
- c. Flow-through entity
- d. Commercial paper

22. In financial accounting, a _____ or Statement of cash flows is a financial statement that shows a company's flow of cash. The money coming into the business is called cash inflow, and money going out from the business is called cash outflow. The statement shows how changes in balance sheet and income accounts affect cash and cash equivalents, and breaks the analysis down to operating, investing, and financing activities.
- a. 3M Company
- b. BNSF Railway
- c. Cash flow statement
- d. BMC Software, Inc.

Chapter 12. Multinational Accounting: Translation of Foreign Entity Statements

23. An _____ allows a company to provide a monetary value for items that make up their inventory. Inventories are usually the largest current asset of a business, and proper measurement of them is necessary to assure accurate financial statements. If inventory is not properly measured, expenses and revenues cannot be properly matched and a company could make poor business decisions.
   a. ABC Television Network
   b. AMEX
   c. Inventory valuation
   d. AIG

24. In finance, _____ is the process of estimating the potential market value of a financial asset or liability. They can be done on assets (for example, investments in marketable securities such as stocks, options, business enterprises, or intangible assets such as patents and trademarks) or on liabilities (e.g., Bonds issued by a company.) A _____ is required in many contexts including investment analysis, capital budgeting, merger and acquisition transactions, financial reporting, taxable events to determine the proper tax liability, and in litigation.
   a. Disclosure
   b. Daybook
   c. Vyborg Appeal
   d. Valuation

25. An _____ is a tax levied on the financial income of people, corporations, or other legal entities. Various _____ systems exist, with varying degrees of tax incidence. Income taxation can be progressive, proportional, or regressive.
   a. Individual Retirement Arrangement
   b. Ordinary income
   c. Implied level of government service
   d. Income tax

Chapter 13. Segment and Interim Reporting

1. _____ means the giving out of information, either voluntarily or to be in compliance with legal regulations or workplace rules.

    - In Computer security, full _____ means disclosing full information about vulnerabilities.
    - In computing, _____ widget
    - Journalism, full _____ refers to disclosing the interests of the writer which may bear on the subject being written about, for example, if the writer has worked with an interview subject in the past.

    - In law:
        - The law of England and Wales, _____ refers to a process that may form part of legal proceedings, whereby parties inform to other parties the existence of any relevant documents that are, or have been, in their control. This compares with the process known as discovery in the course of legal proceedings in the United States.
        - In U.S. civil procedure (litigation rules for civil cases), _____ is a stage prior to trial. In civil cases, each party must disclose to the opposing party the following: names of witnesses which it may use to support its side, copies of documents (or mere description of these documents) in its control which it may use to support its side, computation of damages claimed, and certain insurance information. _____ is related to, but technically prior to, the discovery stage.
        - In Company law (known as 'corporate law' in the United States), _____ refers to giving out information about public or limited companies or their officers, which might be kept secret if the company was a private company or a partnership.

    - In real property transactions, _____ refers to providing to a buyer information known to the seller or broker/agent concerning the condition or other aspects of real property that would affect the property's value or desirability. These rules regarding what information must be disclosed, and whether the information must be disclosed even if a buyer does not ask, vary from one jurisdiction to the next.

    a. Disclosure
    b. Trailing
    c. Controlled Foreign Corporations
    d. Tax harmonisation

2. The _____ is a private, not-for-profit organization whose primary purpose is to develop generally accepted accounting principles (GAAP) within the United States in the public's interest. The Securities and Exchange Commission (SEC) designated the _____ as the organization responsible for setting accounting standards for public companies in the U.S. It was created in 1973, replacing the Accounting Principles Board and the Committee on Accounting Procedure of the American Institute of Certified Public Accountants. The _____'s mission is 'to establish and improve standards of financial accounting and reporting for the guidance and education of the public, including issuers, auditors, and users of financial information.'

    The _____ is not a governmental body.

    a. Governmental Accounting Standards Board
    b. Financial Accounting Standards Board
    c. Fannie Mae
    d. Public company

3. An _____ is a practitioner of accountancy, which is the measurement, disclosure or provision of assurance about financial information that helps managers, investors, tax authorities and other decision makers make resource allocation decisions.

Chapter 13. Segment and Interim Reporting

The word '_____' is derived from the French 'Compter' which took its origin from the Latin 'Computare'. The word was formerly written in English as 'Accomptant', but in process of time the word, which was always pronounced by dropping the 'p', became gradually changed both in pronunciation and in orthography to its present form.

a. ABC Television Network
c. AIG

b. AMEX
d. Accountant

4. The _____ is the umbrella body for the Chartered Accountant profession in Canada and Bermuda. Membership of the CICA totals 70,000 Chartered Accountants and 8,500 students.

Canadian chartered accountants use the designation CA.

a. 3M Company
c. BMC Software, Inc.

b. BNSF Railway
d. Canadian Institute of Chartered Accountants

5. _____ is the title used by members of certain professional accountancy associations in the British Commonwealth countries and Ireland. The term chartered comes from the Royal Charter granted to the world's first professional body of accountants upon their establishment in 1854. The Edinburgh Society of Accountants (formed 1854), the Glasgow Institute of Accountants and Actuaries (1854) and the Aberdeen Society of Accountants (1867) were each granted a royal charter almost from their inception.

a. Chartered Certified Accountant
c. Chartered Accountant

b. Certified General Accountant
d. Certified public accountant

6. The _____ on Company Law was a Company Law Committee, chaired by Lord Jenkins and formed under the tenure of John Rodgers (Parliamentary Secretary to the Board of Trade.) It was formed in November 1959 with terms of reference To review and report upon the provisions and workings of: the Companies Act 1948; the Prevention of Fraud (Investments) Act 1958 and Registration of Business Names Act 1916

Aspects covered included takeovers; the duties of directors and the rights of shareholders

In January 1960 the committee invited comment on a range of subjects including: Incorporation of Companies and Memoranda of Association.

It reported in 1962.

a. Corporate governance
c. Common stock dividend

b. Scottish Poor Laws
d. Jenkins Committee

7. In business and accounting, _____ are everything of value that is owned by a person or company. It is a claim on the property your income of a borrower. The balance sheet of a firm records the monetary value of the _____ owned by the firm.

a. Accounts receivable
b. Assets
c. Earnings before interest, taxes, depreciation and amortization
d. Accrual basis accounting

8. A _____, also client, buyer or purchaser is the buyer or user of the paid products of an individual or organization, mostly called the supplier or seller. This is typically through purchasing or renting goods or services.
   a. 3M Company
   b. BMC Software, Inc.
   c. BNSF Railway
   d. Customer

9. _____ are formal records of a business' financial activities.

In British English, including United Kingdom company law, _____ are often referred to as accounts, although the term _____ is also used, particularly by accountants.

_____ provide an overview of a business' financial condition in both short and long term.

   a. 3M Company
   b. Notes to the financial statements
   c. Statement of retained earnings
   d. Financial statements

10. An _____ is a tax levied on the financial income of people, corporations, or other legal entities. Various _____ systems exist, with varying degrees of tax incidence. Income taxation can be progressive, proportional, or regressive.
    a. Individual Retirement Arrangement
    b. Implied level of government service
    c. Income Tax
    d. Ordinary income

11. In economics, business, retail, and accounting, a _____ is the value of money that has been used up to produce something, and hence is not available for use anymore. In economics, a _____ is an alternative that is given up as a result of a decision. In business, the _____ may be one of acquisition, in which case the amount of money expended to acquire it is counted as _____.
    a. Prime cost
    b. Cost allocation
    c. Cost of quality
    d. Cost

12. In financial accounting, _____ or cost of sales includes the direct costs attributable to the production of the goods sold by a company. This amount includes the materials cost used in creating the goods along with the direct labor costs used to produce the good. It excludes indirect expenses such as distribution costs and sales force costs.
    a. Reorder point
    b. 3M Company
    c. FIFO and LIFO accounting
    d. Cost of goods sold

Chapter 13. Segment and Interim Reporting

13. _____ is the balance of the amounts of cash being received and paid by a business during a defined period of time, sometimes tied to a specific project. Measurement of _____ can be used

- to evaluate the state or performance of a business or project.
- to determine problems with liquidity. Being profitable does not necessarily mean being liquid. A company can fail because of a shortage of cash, even while profitable.
- to project rate of returns. The time of _____s into and out of projects are used as inputs to financial models such as internal rate of return, and net present value.
- to examine income or growth of a business when it is believed that accrual accounting concepts do not represent economic realities. Alternately, _____ can be used to 'validate' the net income generated by accrual accounting.

_____ as a generic term may be used differently depending on context, and certain _____ definitions may be adapted by analysts and users for their own uses. Common terms include operating _____ and free _____.

a. Commercial paper
b. Flow-through entity
c. Controlling interest
d. Cash flow

14. A _____ is a hedge of the exposure to the variability of cash flow that

1. is attributable to a particular risk associated with a recognized asset or liability. Such as all or some future interest payments on variable rate debt or a highly probable forecast transaction and
2. could affect profit or loss

a. Cash flow hedge
b. 3M Company
c. Currency risk
d. Credit risk

15. _____ refers to a business or organization attempting to acquire goods or services to accomplish the goals of the enterprise. Though there are several organizations that attempt to set standards in the _____ process, processes can vary greatly between organizations. Typically the word e;_____e; is not used interchangeably with the word e;procuremente;, since procurement typically includes Expediting, Supplier Quality, and Traffic and Logistics (T'L) in addition to _____.

a. Consignor
b. Supply chain
c. Purchasing
d. Free port

16. _____ methods are means of managing inventory and financial matters involving the money a company ties up within inventory of produced goods, raw materials, parts, components, or feed stocks. FIFO stands for first-in, first-out, meaning that the oldest inventory items are recorded as sold first. LIFO stands for last-in, first-out, meaning that the most recently purchased items are recorded as sold first.

a. 3M Company
b. FIFO and LIFO accounting
c. Finished good
d. Reorder point

Chapter 13. Segment and Interim Reporting

17. In law, _____ refers to the process by which a company (or part of a company) is brought to an end, and the assets and property of the company redistributed. _____ can also be referred to as winding-up or dissolution, although dissolution technically refers to the last stage of _____. The process of _____ also arises when customs, an authority or agency in a country responsible for collecting and safeguarding customs duties, determines the final computation or ascertainment of the duties or drawback accruing on an entry.
   a. BMC Software, Inc.
   b. Liquidation
   c. Bankruptcy protection
   d. 3M Company

18. A _____ is any one of a variety of different systems, institutions, procedures, social relations and infrastructures whereby persons trade, and goods and services are exchanged, forming part of the economy. It is an arrangement that allows buyers and sellers to exchange things. _____s vary in size, range, geographic scale, location, types and variety of human communities, as well as the types of goods and services traded.
   a. Recession
   b. Perfect competition
   c. Market Failure
   d. Market

19. The _____ is the former authoritative body of the American Institute of Certified Public Accountants (AICPA.) It was created by the American Institute of Certified Public Accountants in 1959 and issued pronouncements on accounting principles until 1973, when it was replaced by the Financial Accounting Standards Board (FASB.)

The _____ was disbanded in the hopes that the smaller, fully-independent FASB could more effectively create accounting standards.

   a. International Federation of Accountants
   b. Institute of Management Accountants
   c. American Payroll Association
   d. Accounting Principles Board

20. _____ is a form of corporation equity ownership represented in the securities. It is a stock whose dividends are based on market fluctuations. It is dangerous in comparison to preferred shares and some other investment options, in that in the event of bankruptcy, _____ investors receive their funds after preferred stock holders, bondholders, creditors, etc. On the other hand, common shares on average perform better than preferred shares or bonds over time.
   a. Stock split
   b. 3M Company
   c. Common Stock
   d. Growth investing

21. _____ in accounting is the process of treating equity investments, usually 20-50%, in associate companies. The investor keeps such equities as an asset. Proportional share of associate company's net income increases the investment, and proportional payment of dividends decreases it.
   a. AIG
   b. ABC Television Network
   c. Equity Method
   d. Out-of-pocket

Chapter 14. SEC Reporting

1. The _____ is an elected body forming part of the City of London Corporation. The _____ is made up of the twenty five Aldermen of the City of London, presided over by the Lord Mayor. The court was originally responsible for the entire administration of the City, but most of its responsibilities were subsumed by the Court of Common Council in the fourteenth century.
   a. BMC Software, Inc.
   b. BNSF Railway
   c. Court of Aldermen
   d. 3M Company

2. The _____ of 1977 (15 U.S.C. §§ 78dd-1, et seq.) is a United States federal law known primarily for two of its main provisions, one that addresses accounting transparency requirements under the Securities Exchange Act of 1934 and another concerning bribery of foreign officials.
   a. Lease
   b. Competition law
   c. Foreign Corrupt Practices Act
   d. Pre-emption right

3. _____ is an equity (stock) exchange located at 11 Wall Street in lower Manhattan, New York, USA.) It is the largest stock exchange in the world by dollar value of its listed companies' securities. As of October 2008, the combined capitalization of all domestic _____ listed companies was US$10.1 trillion.
   a. BNSF Railway
   b. 3M Company
   c. New York Stock Exchange
   d. BMC Software, Inc.

4. A _____ is a fungible, negotiable instrument representing financial value. they are broadly categorized into debt securities (such as banknotes, bonds and debentures), and equity securities; e.g., common stocks. The company or other entity issuing the _____ is called the issuer.
   a. 3M Company
   b. BMC Software, Inc.
   c. Security
   d. Tracking stock

5. The U.S. _____ is an independent agency of the United States government which holds primary responsibility for enforcing the federal securities laws and regulating the securities industry, the nation's stock and options exchanges, and other electronic securities markets. The SEC was created by section 4 of the Securities Exchange Act of 1934 (now codified as 15 U.S.C. § 78d and commonly referred to as the 1934 Act.)
   a. BNSF Railway
   b. Securities and Exchange Commission
   c. BMC Software, Inc.
   d. 3M Company

6. A _____, (formerly a securities exchange) is a corporation or mutual organization which provides 'trading' facilities for stock brokers and traders, to trade stocks and other securities. _____s also provide facilities for the issue and redemption of securities as well as other financial instruments and capital events including the payment of income and dividends. The securities traded on a _____ include: shares issued by companies, unit trusts, derivatives, pooled investment products and bonds.
   a. BNSF Railway
   b. 3M Company
   c. BMC Software, Inc.
   d. Stock Exchange

7. _____, the Electronic Data-Gathering, Analysis, and Retrieval system, performs automated collection, validation, indexing, acceptance, and forwarding of submissions by companies and others who are required by law to file forms with the U.S. Securities and Exchange Commission (the 'SEC'.) The database is freely available to the public via Web or FTP, typically posting in excess of 3,000 filings per day.

Not all SEC filings by public companies are available on _____.

a. AMEX	b. ABC Television Network
c. AIG	d. EDGAR

8. The _____ was a worldwide economic downturn starting in most places in 1929 and ending at different times in the 1930s or early 1940s for different countries. It was the largest and most important economic depression in the 20th century, and is used in the 21st century as an example of how far the world's economy can fall. The _____ originated in the United States; historians most often use as a starting date the stock market crash on October 29, 1929, known as Black Tuesday.

a. Great Depression	b. BNSF Railway
c. 3M Company	d. BMC Software, Inc.

9. Congress enacted the _____, in the aftermath of the stock market crash of 1929 and during the ensuing Great Depression.

a. Bookkeeping	b. Sustainability measurement
c. Securities Act of 1933	d. Monte Carlo methods

10. The _____ of 1934 is a law governing the secondary trading of securities (stocks, bonds, and debentures) in the United States of America. The Act, 48 Stat. 881 (enacted June 6, 1934), codified at 15 U.S.C.

a. BNSF Railway	b. BMC Software, Inc.
c. 3M Company	d. Securities Exchange Act

11. The _____ is a law governing the secondary trading of securities (stocks, bonds, and debentures) in the United States of America. The Act, 48 Stat. 881 (enacted June 6, 1934), codified at 15 U.S.C.

a. BNSF Railway	b. 3M Company
c. BMC Software, Inc.	d. Securities Exchange Act of 1934

12. The _____ is an international organization that brings together the regulators of the world's securities and futures markets. It, along with its sister organizations, the Basel Committee on Banking Supervision and the International Association of Insurance Supervisors, together make up the Joint Forum of international financial regulators. Currently, _____ members regulate more than 90 percent of the world's securities markets.

a. AIG	b. ABC Television Network
c. AMEX	d. International Organization of Securities Commissions

13. The _____ founded on April 1, 2001 is the successor of the International Accounting Standards Committee (IASC) founded in June 1973 in London. It is responsible for developing the International Financial Reporting Standards (new name for the International Accounting Standards issued after 2001), and promoting the use and application of these standards.

The _____ is an independent, privately-funded accounting standard-setter based in London, UK.

a. Institute of Management Accountants	b. Information Systems Audit and Control Association
c. Emerging technologies	d. International Accounting Standards Board

14. An _____ is a mostly hierarchical concept of subordination of entities that collaborate and contribute to serve one common aim.

Chapter 14. SEC Reporting

Organizations are a variant of clustered entities. The structure of an organization is usually set up in many a styles, dependent on their objectives and ambience.

a. AIG
b. ABC Television Network
c. AMEX
d. Organizational structure

15. An _____ is a legal contract between two parties, particularly for indentured labour or a term of apprenticeship but also for certain land transactions. The term comes from the medieval English '_____ of retainer' -- a legal contract written in duplicate on the same sheet, with the copies separated by cutting along a jagged line so that the teeth of the two parts could later be refitted to confirm authenticity. Each party to the deed would then retain a part.
a. Employee Retirement Income Security Act
b. Indenture
c. Operating Lease
d. Impracticability

16. The _____, codified at 15 U.S.C. §§ 80b-1 through 15 U.S.C. §§ 80b-21, is a United States federal law that was created to regulate the actions of investment advisers (also spelled 'advisors') as defined by the law.
a. Investment Advisers Act of 1940
b. Express warranty
c. Exclusive right
d. Independent contractor

17. An _____ is a company whose main business is holding securities of other companies purely for investment purposes. The _____ invests money on behalf of its shareholders who in turn share in the profits and losses.

In United States securities law, there are at least three types of investment companies :

- Open-End Management Investment Companies (mutual funds)
- Closed-End Management Investment Companies (closed-end funds)
- UITs (unit investment trusts)

A fourth and lesser-known type of _____ under the _____ Act of 1940 is a Face-Amount Certificate Company.

a. ABC Television Network
b. Investment Company
c. AIG
d. AMEX

18. The _____ is an act of Congress. It was passed as a United States Public Law (PL-768) on August 22, 1940, and is codified at 15 U.S.C. §§ 80a-1 through 15 U.S.C.
a. AMEX
b. Investment Company Act of 1940
c. ABC Television Network
d. AIG

19. A _____ is any one of a variety of different systems, institutions, procedures, social relations and infrastructures whereby persons trade, and goods and services are exchanged, forming part of the economy. It is an arrangement that allows buyers and sellers to exchange things. _____s vary in size, range, geographic scale, location, types and variety of human communities, as well as the types of goods and services traded.
a. Market
b. Recession
c. Market Failure
d. Perfect competition

Chapter 14. SEC Reporting

20. The _____ is a federally mandated non-profit corporation in the United States that protects securities investors from financial harm if a broker-dealer company fails. Investors are not insured for any potential loss while invested in the securities market.

The United States Congress created _____ in 1970 through the _____ (15 U.S.C.

a. BMC Software, Inc.
b. 3M Company
c. BNSF Railway
d. SIPC

21. The _____ is a federally mandated non-profit corporation in the United States that protects securities investors from financial harm if a broker-dealer company fails. Investors are not insured for any potential loss while invested in the securities market.

The United States Congress created _____ in 1970 through the Securities Investor Protection Act (15 U.S.C.

a. BNSF Railway
b. BMC Software, Inc.
c. Securities Investor Protection Corporation
d. 3M Company

22. The United States _____ Act of 1939 (Trust indentureA), codified at 15 U.S.C. § 77aaa through 15 U.S.C. § 77bbbb, supplements the Securities Act of 1933 in the case of the distribution of debt securities.

a. Trust Indenture
b. Robinson-Patman Act
c. Covenant
d. Charter

23. The United States _____, codified at 15 U.S.C. § 77aaa through 15 U.S.C. § 77bbbb, supplements the Securities Act of 1933 in the case of the distribution of debt securities.

a. Lease
b. Burden of proof
c. Trust Indenture Act of 1939
d. Coming into force

24. _____ is a legally declared inability or impairment of ability of an individual or organization to pay its creditors. Creditors may file a _____ petition against a debtor ('involuntary _____') in an effort to recoup a portion of what they are owed or initiate a restructuring. In the majority of cases, however, _____ is initiated by the debtor (a 'voluntary _____' that is filed by the bankrupt individual or organization.)

a. BMC Software, Inc.
b. 3M Company
c. Bankruptcy protection
d. Bankruptcy

25. _____ is the set of processes, customs, policies, laws, and institutions affecting the way a corporation is directed, administered or controlled. _____ also includes the relationships among the many stakeholders involved and the goals for which the corporation is governed. The principal stakeholders are the shareholders/members, management, and the board of directors.

a. Trust indenture
b. FLSA
c. Corporate governance
d. Patent

Chapter 14. SEC Reporting

26. The _____ is a private, not-for-profit organization whose primary purpose is to develop generally accepted accounting principles (GAAP) within the United States in the public's interest. The Securities and Exchange Commission (SEC) designated the _____ as the organization responsible for setting accounting standards for public companies in the U.S. It was created in 1973, replacing the Accounting Principles Board and the Committee on Accounting Procedure of the American Institute of Certified Public Accountants. The _____'s mission is 'to establish and improve standards of financial accounting and reporting for the guidance and education of the public, including issuers, auditors, and users of financial information.'

The _____ is not a governmental body.

a. Financial Accounting Standards Board
b. Public company
c. Fannie Mae
d. Governmental Accounting Standards Board

27. The _____ of 2002 (Pub.L. 107-204, 116 Stat. 745, enacted July 30, 2002), also known as the Public Company Accounting Reform and Investor Protection Act of 2002, is a United States federal law enacted on July 30, 2002 in response to a number of major corporate and accounting scandals including those affecting Enron, Tyco International, Adelphia, Peregrine Systems and WorldCom. The legislation establishes new or enhanced standards for all U.S. public company boards, management, and public accounting firms. It does not apply to privately held companies.

a. Lease
b. Fair Labor Standards Act
c. FCPA
d. Sarbanes-Oxley Act

28. In finance, a _____ is a debt security, in which the authorized issuer owes the holders a debt and, depending on the terms of the _____, is obliged to pay interest (the coupon) and/or to repay the principal at a later date, termed maturity. It is a formal contract to repay borrowed money with interest at fixed intervals.

Thus a _____ is like a loan: the issuer is the borrower, the _____ holder is the lender, and the coupon is the interest.

a. Zero-coupon bond
b. Revenue bonds
c. Bond
d. Coupon rate

29. An _____ is the buying of one company by another. An _____ may be friendly or hostile. In the former case, the companies cooperate in negotiations; in the latter case, the takeover target is unwilling to be bought or the target's board has no prior knowledge of the offer. _____ usually refers to a purchase of a smaller firm by a larger one. Sometimes, however, a smaller firm will acquire management control of a larger or longer established company and keep its name for the combined entity. This is known as a reverse takeover.

a. AMEX
b. Acquisition
c. ABC Television Network
d. AIG

Chapter 14. SEC Reporting

30. _____ means the giving out of information, either voluntarily or to be in compliance with legal regulations or workplace rules.

- In Computer security, full _____ means disclosing full information about vulnerabilities.
- In computing, _____ widget
- Journalism, full _____ refers to disclosing the interests of the writer which may bear on the subject being written about, for example, if the writer has worked with an interview subject in the past.

- In law:
  - The law of England and Wales, _____ refers to a process that may form part of legal proceedings, whereby parties inform to other parties the existence of any relevant documents that are, or have been, in their control. This compares with the process known as discovery in the course of legal proceedings in the United States.
  - In U.S. civil procedure (litigation rules for civil cases), _____ is a stage prior to trial. In civil cases, each party must disclose to the opposing party the following: names of witnesses which it may use to support its side, copies of documents (or mere description of these documents) in its control which it may use to support its side, computation of damages claimed, and certain insurance information. _____ is related to, but technically prior to, the discovery stage.
  - In Company law (known as 'corporate law' in the United States), _____ refers to giving out information about public or limited companies or their officers, which might be kept secret if the company was a private company or a partnership.

- In real property transactions, _____ refers to providing to a buyer information known to the seller or broker/agent concerning the condition or other aspects of real property that would affect the property's value or desirability. These rules regarding what information must be disclosed, and whether the information must be disclosed even if a buyer does not ask, vary from one jurisdiction to the next.

a. Controlled Foreign Corporations
c. Trailing
b. Tax harmonisation
d. Disclosure

31. In financial accounting, a _____ is defined as an obligation of an entity arising from past transactions or events, the settlement of which may result in the transfer or use of assets, provision of services or other yielding of economic benefits in the future.

a. False Claims Act
c. Vested
b. Liability
d. Corporate governance

32. _____ is an arrangement with the U.S. Securities and Exchange Commission that allows a single registration document to be filed that permits the issuance of multiple securities.

_____ is a registration of a new issue which can be prepared up to two years in advance, so that the issue can be offered quickly as soon as funds are needed or market conditions are favorable.

For example, current market conditions in the housing market are not favorable for a specific firm to issue a public offering.

Chapter 14. SEC Reporting

a. BMC Software, Inc.
c. BNSF Railway
b. 3M Company
d. Shelf registration

33. An _____ is a practitioner of accountancy, which is the measurement, disclosure or provision of assurance about financial information that helps managers, investors, tax authorities and other decision makers make resource allocation decisions.

The word '_____' is derived from the French 'Compter' which took its origin from the Latin 'Computare'. The word was formerly written in English as 'Accomptant', but in process of time the word, which was always pronounced by dropping the 'p', became gradually changed both in pronunciation and in orthography to its present form.

a. ABC Television Network
c. AMEX
b. AIG
d. Accountant

34. Initial _____, also referred to simply as a '_____' or 'flotation,' is when a company issues common stock or shares to the public for the first time. They are often issued by smaller, younger companies seeking capital to expand, but can also be done by large privately-owned companies looking to become publicly traded.

In an Ipublic offering the issuer may obtain the assistance of an underwriting firm, which helps it determine what type of security to issue (common or preferred), best offering price and time to bring it to market.

a. Public offering
c. Gross income
b. Restricted stock
d. Commercial paper

35. A _____ is an annual report required by the U.S. Securities and Exchange Commission (SEC), that gives a comprehensive summary of a public company's performance. Although similarly named, the annual report on _____ is distinct from the often glossy 'annual report to shareholders', which a company must send to its shareholders when it holds an annual meeting to elect directors (though some companies combine the annual report and the 10-K into one document.) The 10-K includes information such as company history, organizational structure, executive compensation, equity, subsidiaries, and audited financial statements, among other information.

a. Form 10-Q
c. Form 10-K
b. Form 8-K
d. 3M Company

36. _____, Quarterly Report Pursuant to Section 13 or 15(d) of the Securities Exchange Act of 1934, is an SEC filing that must be filed quarterly with the US Securities and Exchange Commission. It contains similar information to the annual form 10-K, however the information is generally less detailed, and the financial statements are generally unaudited. Information for the final quarter of a firm's fiscal year is included in the 10-K, so only three 10-Q filings are made each year.

a. 3M Company
c. Form 20-F
b. Form 8-K
d. Form 10-Q

37. _____ is a report required to be filed by public companies with the United States Securities and Exchange Commission pursuant to the Securities Exchange Act of 1934, as amended. After a significant event like bankruptcy or departure of a CEO, a public company generally must file a Current Report on _____ within four business days to provide an update to previously filed quartely reports on Form 10-Q and/or Annual Reports on Form 10-K. _____ is a very broad form used to notify investors of any unscheduled material event that is important to shareholders or the SEC.

a. 3M Company
c. Form 10-Q
b. Form 20-F
d. Form 8-K

38. The _____ (sometimes called 'Peekaboo') is a private-sector, non-profit corporation created by the Sarbanes-Oxley Act, a 2002 United States federal law, to oversee the auditors of public companies. Its stated purpose is to 'protect the interests of investors and further the public interest in the preparation of informative, fair, and independent audit reports'. Although a private entity, the _____ has many government-like regulatory functions, making it in some ways similar to the private Self Regulatory Organizations (SROs) that regulate stock markets and other aspects of the financial markets in the United States.

a. 3M Company
c. Pension Benefit Guaranty Corporation
b. Financial Crimes Enforcement Network
d. Public Company Accounting Oversight Board

39. The term _____ usually refers to a company that is permitted to offer its registered securities (stock, bonds, etc.) for sale to the general public, typically through a stock exchange, or occasionally a company whose stock is traded over the counter (OTC) via market makers who use non-exchange quotation services.

The term '_____' may also refer to a company owned by the government.

a. MicroStrategy
c. Public Company
b. Governmental Accounting Standards Board
d. Professional association

40. A _____ is the pinnacle activity involved in selling products or services in return for money or other compensation. It is an act of completion of a commercial activity.

A _____ is completed by the seller, the owner of the goods.

a. Tertiary sector of economy
c. Maturity
b. High yield stock
d. Sale

41. The general definition of an _____ is an evaluation of a person, organization, system, process, project or product. _____s are performed to ascertain the validity and reliability of information; also to provide an assessment of a system's internal control. The goal of an _____ is to express an opinion on the person/organization/system (etc) in question, under evaluation based on work done on a test basis.

a. Assurance service
c. Audit
b. Institute of Chartered Accountants of India
d. Audit regime

42. In a publicly-held company, an _____ is an operating committee of the Board of Directors, typically charged with oversight of financial reporting and disclosure. Committee members are drawn from members of the Company's board of directors, with a Chairperson selected from among the members. An _____ of a publicly-traded company in the United States is composed of independent and outside directors referred to as non-executive directors, at least one of which is typically a financial expert.

a. Audit working paper
c. Event data
b. External auditor
d. Audit committee

43. _____ are formal records of a business' financial activities.

Chapter 14. SEC Reporting

In British English, including United Kingdom company law, _____ are often referred to as accounts, although the term _____ is also used, particularly by accountants.

_____ provide an overview of a business' financial condition in both short and long term.

a. Financial statements
b. 3M Company
c. Statement of retained earnings
d. Notes to the financial statements

44. Most patent law systems require that a patent application disclose a claimed invention in sufficient detail for the notional person skilled in the art to carry out that claimed invention. This requirement is often known as sufficiency of disclosure or enablement, depending on the jurisdiction.

The _____ lies at the heart and origin of patent law. A state or government grants an inventor, or the inventor's assignee, a monopoly for a given period of time in exchange for the inventor disclosing to the public how to make or practice his or her invention. If a patent fails to contain such information, then the bargain is violated, and the patent is unenforceable.

a. Tax patent
b. False Claims Act
c. Pre-emption right
d. Disclosure requirement

45. _____ is generally understood in financial circles as the point at which revenue is recognized, typically through a transaction which involves the exchange of an asset, product, or service for cash or its equivalents.

This approach gives the accounting division a strictly objective basis for changing the books. For example, a homeowner may believe that his house has grown in value during a strong market, or fallen in value during a weak market, but until the house is actually sold for a specific price to a specific buyer, the change in value can only be estimated and is considered unrealized.

a. Realization
b. Merck ' Co., Inc.
c. Valuation
d. Total-factor productivity

46. _____ Corporation of America was a Los Angeles-based U.S. financial conglomerate that marketed a package of mutual funds and life insurance to private individuals in the 1960s and 70s. It collapsed in scandal in 1973 after ex-employee Ronald Secrist and securities analyst Ray Dirks blew the whistle on massive accounting fraud, including a computer system dedicated exclusively to creating and maintaining fictitious insurance policies. Investigation found that from 1964 onward, as many as 100 company employees had engaged in organized deception of investors, auditors, reinsurers and regulatory authorities.

a. ABC Television Network
b. AMEX
c. AIG
d. Equity Funding

47. _____ are ten auditing standards, developed by the AICPA, consisting of general standards, standards of field work, and standards of reporting, along with interpretations. They were developed by the AICPA in 1947 and have undergone minor changes since then.

The _____ are as follows:

1. The auditor must have adequate technical training and proficiency to perform the audit
2. The auditor must maintain independence in mental attitude in all matters related to the audit.
3. The auditor must use due professional care during the performance of the audit and the preparation of the report.

1. The auditor must adequately plan the work and must properly supervise any assistants.
2. The auditor must obtain a sufficient understanding of the entity and its environment, including its internal control, to assess the risk of material misstatement of the financial statements whether due to error or fraud, and to design the nature, timing, and extent of further audit procedures.
3. The auditor must obtain sufficient appropriate audit evidence by performing audit procedures to afford a reasonable basis for an opinion regarding the financial statements under audit.

The new standards are in effect for audits of financial statements for periods beginning on or after December 15, 2006.

1. The auditor must state in the auditor's report whether the financial statements are in accordance with generally accepted accounting principles (GAAP.)
2. The auditor must identify in the auditor's report those circumstances in which such principles have not been consistently observed in the current period in relation to the preceding period.
3. When the auditor determines that informative disclosures are not reasonably adequate, the auditor must so state in the auditor's report.
4. The auditor must either express an opinion regarding the financial statements, taken as a whole the auditor should state the reasons therefore in the auditor's report. In all cases where the auditor's name is associated with the financial statements, the auditor should clearly indicate the character of the auditor's work, if any, and the degree of responsibility the auditor is taking, in the auditor's report.

a. Generally accepted auditing standards
b. Joint audit
c. Negative assurance
d. Continuous auditing

Chapter 15. Partnerships: Formation, Operation, and Changes in Membership 79

1. A _____ is a type of business entity in which partners (owners) share with each other the profits or losses of the business undertaking in which all have invested. _____s are often favored over corporations for taxation purposes, as the _____ structure does not generally incur a tax on profits before it is distributed to the partners (i.e. there is no dividend tax levied.) However, depending on the _____ structure and the jurisdiction in which it operates, owners of a _____ may be exposed to greater personal liability than they would as shareholders of a corporation.
   a. Corporate governance
   b. Partnership
   c. Resource Conservation and Recovery Act
   d. National Information Infrastructure Protection Act

2. The _____ , which includes revisions that are sometimes called the Revised _____, is a uniform act (similar to a model statute), proposed by the National Conference of Commissioners on Uniform State Laws ('NCCUSL') for the governance of business partnerships by U.S. States. Several versions of _____ have been promulgated by the NCCUSL, the earliest having been put forth in 1914, and the most recent in 1997.

The NCCUSL's first revision of _____ was promulgated in 1992 and amended in 1993 and 1994.

   a. ABC Television Network
   b. AIG
   c. Uniform Partnership Act
   d. AMEX

3. In the commercial and legal parlance of most countries, a _____ or simply a partnership, refers to an association of persons or an unincorporated company with the following major features:

   - Created by agreement, proof of existence and estoppel.
   - Formed by two or more persons
   - The owners are all personally liable for any legal actions and debts the company may face

It is a partnership in which partners share equally in both responsibility and liability.

Partnerships have certain default characteristics relating to both the relationship between the individual partners and (b) the relationship between the partnership and the outside world. The former can generally be overridden by agreement between the partners, whereas the latter generally cannot be.

The assets of the business are owned on behalf of the other partners, and they are each personally liable, jointly and severally, for business debts, taxes or tortious liability.

   a. Governmental Accounting Standards Board
   b. Dow Jones ' Company
   c. Multinational corporation
   d. General partnership

4. _____ is a concept whereby a person's financial liability is limited to a fixed sum, most commonly the value of a person's investment in a company or partnership with _____. A shareholder in a limited company is not personally liable for any of the debts of the company, other than for the value of his investment in that company. The same is true for the members of a _____ partnership and the limited partners in a limited partnership.
   a. Due diligence
   b. Burden of proof
   c. Joint venture
   d. Limited liability

5. A _____ is a partnership in which some or all partners (depending on the jurisdiction) have limited liability. It therefore exhibits elements of partnerships and corporations. In an _____ one partner is not responsible or liable for another partner's misconduct or negligence.

Chapter 15. Partnerships: Formation, Operation, and Changes in Membership

a. Dow Jones ' Company
c. Limited liability partnership
b. Financial Accounting Standards Board
d. Privately held

6. A _____ is a form of partnership similar to a general partnership, except that in addition to one or more general partners (GPs), there are one or more limited partners (_____s.) It is a partnership in which only one partner is required to be a general partner.

The GPs are, in all major respects, in the same legal position as partners in a conventional firm, i.e. they have management control, share the right to use partnership property, share the profits of the firm in predefined proportions, and have joint and several liability for the debts of the partnership.

a. Debenture
c. Minority interest
b. Limited partnership
d. Dow Jones ' Company

7. In financial accounting, a _____ is defined as an obligation of an entity arising from past transactions or events, the settlement of which may result in the transfer or use of assets, provision of services or other yielding of economic benefits in the future.

a. Vested
c. Liability
b. Corporate governance
d. False Claims Act

8. The _____ is a non-profit, unincorporated association in the United States that consists of commissioners appointed by each state and territory. The purpose of the association is to discuss and debate in which areas of law there should be uniformity among the states and to draft acts accordingly (called Uniform Acts.) The results of these discussions are proposed to the states as either model acts or uniform acts.

a. Dow Jones ' Company
c. HFMA
b. Limited liability partnership
d. National Conference of Commissioners on Uniform State Laws

9. The Uniform Limited Partnership Act (ULPA), which includes its 1976 revision called the _____ (RULPA), is a uniform act (similar to a model statute), proposed by the National Conference of Commissioners on Uniform State Laws ('NCCUSL') for the governance of business partnerships by U.S. States. The NCCUSL promulgated the original ULPA in 1916 and the most recent revision in 2001.

The NCCUSL promulgated the original ULPA in 1916, which is now called the Uniform Limited Partnership Act (1916) or ULPA (1916); a 1976 revision named the _____ which is also now called the Uniform Limited Partnership Act (1976), ULPA (1976) or _____ (1976); a 1985 revision named Uniform Limited Partnership Act (1976) with 1985 Amendments, which is also now called ULPA (1985) or _____ (1985); and a 2001 revision that was colloquially called Re-_____ during the drafting process but then was officially named the Uniform Limited Partnership Act (2001) or ULPA (2001.)

a. 3M Company
c. BMC Software, Inc.
b. RULPA
d. BNSF Railway

Chapter 15. Partnerships: Formation, Operation, and Changes in Membership 81

10. In economics, _____ or _____ goods or real _____ refers to factors of production used to create goods or services that are not themselves significantly consumed (though they may depreciate) in the production process. _____ goods may be acquired with money or financial _____. In finance and accounting, _____ generally refers to financial wealth, especially that used to start or maintain a business.
   a. Disclosure
   b. Capital
   c. Vyborg Appeal
   d. Screening

11. A _____ is a type of debt Like all debt instruments, a _____ entails the redistribution of financial assets over time, between the lender and the borrower.
   a. Loan to value
   b. Lender
   c. Loan
   d. Debenture

12. _____ is a fee paid on borrowed assets. It is the price paid for the use of borrowed money, or, money earned by deposited funds. Assets that are sometimes lent with _____ include money, shares, consumer goods through hire purchase, major assets such as aircraft, and even entire factories in finance lease arrangements. The _____ is calculated upon the value of the assets in the same manner as upon money.
   a. Insolvency
   b. ABC Television Network
   c. AIG
   d. Interest

13. _____ are formal records of a business' financial activities.

In British English, including United Kingdom company law, _____ are often referred to as accounts, although the term _____ is also used, particularly by accountants.

_____ provide an overview of a business' financial condition in both short and long term.

   a. Notes to the financial statements
   b. 3M Company
   c. Financial statements
   d. Statement of retained earnings

14. In business and accounting, _____ are everything of value that is owned by a person or company. It is a claim on the property your income of a borrower. The balance sheet of a firm records the monetary value of the _____ owned by the firm.
   a. Accrual basis accounting
   b. Assets
   c. Earnings before interest, taxes, depreciation and amortization
   d. Accounts receivable

15. In finance, _____ is the process of estimating the potential market value of a financial asset or liability. They can be done on assets (for example, investments in marketable securities such as stocks, options, business enterprises, or intangible assets such as patents and trademarks) or on liabilities (e.g., Bonds issued by a company.) A _____ is required in many contexts including investment analysis, capital budgeting, merger and acquisition transactions, financial reporting, taxable events to determine the proper tax liability, and in litigation.
   a. Vyborg Appeal
   b. Valuation
   c. Daybook
   d. Disclosure

Chapter 15. Partnerships: Formation, Operation, and Changes in Membership

16. In accounting, _____ or carrying value is the value of an asset according to its balance sheet account balance. For assets, the value is based on the original cost of the asset less any depreciation, amortization or impairment costs made against the asset. Traditionally, a company's _____ is its total assets minus intangible assets and liabilities.
    a. Depreciation
    b. Matching principle
    c. Book value
    d. Generally accepted accounting principles

17. In economics, business, retail, and accounting, a _____ is the value of money that has been used up to produce something, and hence is not available for use anymore. In economics, a _____ is an alternative that is given up as a result of a decision. In business, the _____ may be one of acquisition, in which case the amount of money expended to acquire it is counted as _____.
    a. Prime cost
    b. Cost
    c. Cost allocation
    d. Cost of quality

18. In law, _____ refers to the process by which a company (or part of a company) is brought to an end, and the assets and property of the company redistributed. _____ can also be referred to as winding-up or dissolution, although dissolution technically refers to the last stage of _____. The process of _____ also arises when customs, an authority or agency in a country responsible for collecting and safeguarding customs duties, determines the final computation or ascertainment of the duties or drawback accruing on an entry.
    a. Bankruptcy protection
    b. Liquidation
    c. 3M Company
    d. BMC Software, Inc.

19. The _____ is a private, not-for-profit organization whose primary purpose is to develop generally accepted accounting principles (GAAP) within the United States in the public's interest. The Securities and Exchange Commission (SEC) designated the _____ as the organization responsible for setting accounting standards for public companies in the U.S. It was created in 1973, replacing the Accounting Principles Board and the Committee on Accounting Procedure of the American Institute of Certified Public Accountants. The _____'s mission is 'to establish and improve standards of financial accounting and reporting for the guidance and education of the public, including issuers, auditors, and users of financial information.'

    The _____ is not a governmental body.

    a. Financial Accounting Standards Board
    b. Governmental Accounting Standards Board
    c. Fannie Mae
    d. Public company

20. _____ are defined as identifiable non-monetary assets that cannot be seen, touched or physically measured, which are created through time and/or effort and that are identifiable as a separate asset. There are two primary forms of intangibles - legal intangibles (such as trade secrets (e.g., customer lists), copyrights, patents, trademarks, and goodwill) and competitive intangibles (such as knowledge activities (know-how, knowledge), collaboration activities, leverage activities, and structural activities.) Legal intangibles are known under the generic term intellectual property and generate legal property rights defensible in a court of law.
    a. Intangible assets
    b. ABC Television Network
    c. AIG
    d. Overhead

21. An _____ is a tax levied on the financial income of people, corporations, or other legal entities. Various _____ systems exist, with varying degrees of tax incidence. Income taxation can be progressive, proportional, or regressive.

Chapter 15. Partnerships: Formation, Operation, and Changes in Membership 83

a. Ordinary income
c. Implied level of government service

b. Individual Retirement Arrangement
d. Income tax

22. The _____ is the former authoritative body of the American Institute of Certified Public Accountants (AICPA.) It was created by the American Institute of Certified Public Accountants in 1959 and issued pronouncements on accounting principles until 1973, when it was replaced by the Financial Accounting Standards Board (FASB.)

The _____ was disbanded in the hopes that the smaller, fully-independent FASB could more effectively create accounting standards.

a. American Payroll Association
c. International Federation of Accountants

b. Accounting Principles Board
d. Institute of Management Accountants

23. _____ is a form of corporation equity ownership represented in the securities. It is a stock whose dividends are based on market fluctuations. It is dangerous in comparison to preferred shares and some other investment options, in that in the event of bankruptcy, _____ investors receive their funds after preferred stock holders, bondholders, creditors, etc. On the other hand, common shares on average perform better than preferred shares or bonds over time.

a. Growth investing
c. Common Stock

b. Stock split
d. 3M Company

24. _____ in accounting is the process of treating equity investments, usually 20-50%, in associate companies. The investor keeps such equities as an asset. Proportional share of associate company's net income increases the investment, and proportional payment of dividends decreases it.

a. ABC Television Network
c. Out-of-pocket

b. AIG
d. Equity Method

25. A _____ is an entity formed between two or more parties to undertake economic activity together. The parties agree to create a new entity by both contributing equity, and they then share in the revenues, expenses, and control of the enterprise. The venture can be for one specific project only, or a continuing business relationship such as the Fuji Xerox _____.

a. Pre-emption right
c. Fraud Enforcement and Recovery Act

b. Chief Financial Officers Act of 1990
d. Joint venture

26. An _____ is a practitioner of accountancy, which is the measurement, disclosure or provision of assurance about financial information that helps managers, investors, tax authorities and other decision makers make resource allocation decisions.

The word '_____' is derived from the French 'Compter' which took its origin from the Latin 'Computare'. The word was formerly written in English as 'Accomptant', but in process of time the word, which was always pronounced by dropping the 'p', became gradually changed both in pronunciation and in orthography to its present form.

a. AIG
c. ABC Television Network

b. AMEX
d. Accountant

Chapter 15. Partnerships: Formation, Operation, and Changes in Membership

27. The _____ is the national, professional association of CPAs in the United States, with more than 330,000 members, including CPAs in business and industry, public practice, government, and education; student affiliates; and international associates. It sets ethical standards for the profession and U.S. auditing standards for audits of private companies; federal, state and local governments; and non-profit organizations.

Approximately 40% of its members are engaged in the practice of public accounting, in areas such as auditing, accounting, taxation, general business consulting, business valuation, personal financial planning and business technology.

   a. ABC Television Network
   b. American Institute of Certified Public Accountants
   c. AIG
   d. Other postemployment benefits

28. _____ is the statutory title of qualified accountants in the United States who have passed the Uniform _____ Examination and have met additional state education and experience requirements for certification as a _____. Individuals who have passed the Exam but have not either accomplished the required on-the-job experience or have previously met it but in the meantime have lapsed their continuing professional education are, in many states, permitted the designation '_____ Inactive' or an equivalent phrase. In most U.S. states, only _____s who are licensed are able to provide to the public attestation (including auditing) opinions on financial statements.

   a. Chartered Accountant
   b. Certified Public Accountant
   c. Certified General Accountant
   d. Chartered Certified Accountant

29. _____, revised and replaced in its entirety by FIN 46R, is a statement for the purposes of United States Generally Accepted Accounting Principles published by the US Financial Accounting Standards Board (FASB) which requires a reporting enterprise to consolidate a variable interest entity (VIE) if it is the primary beneficiary of the VIE based on variable interests. One of the main reasons FIN46 was issued as an interpretation instead of an accounting standard was to issue the standard in a relatively short period of time in response to the Enron scandal.

FIN 46R is an interpretation of ARB 51 relating to consolidation.

   a. BNSF Railway
   b. BMC Software, Inc.
   c. 3M Company
   d. FIN 46

Chapter 16. Partnerships: Liquidation

1. A _____ is a type of business entity in which partners (owners) share with each other the profits or losses of the business undertaking in which all have invested. _____s are often favored over corporations for taxation purposes, as the _____ structure does not generally incur a tax on profits before it is distributed to the partners (i.e. there is no dividend tax levied.) However, depending on the _____ structure and the jurisdiction in which it operates, owners of a _____ may be exposed to greater personal liability than they would as shareholders of a corporation.
    a. National Information Infrastructure Protection Act
    b. Corporate governance
    c. Resource Conservation and Recovery Act
    d. Partnership

2. The _____ , which includes revisions that are sometimes called the Revised _____, is a uniform act (similar to a model statute), proposed by the National Conference of Commissioners on Uniform State Laws ('NCCUSL') for the governance of business partnerships by U.S. States. Several versions of _____ have been promulgated by the NCCUSL, the earliest having been put forth in 1914, and the most recent in 1997.

    The NCCUSL's first revision of _____ was promulgated in 1992 and amended in 1993 and 1994.

    a. ABC Television Network
    b. AMEX
    c. AIG
    d. Uniform Partnership Act

3. In law, _____ refers to the process by which a company (or part of a company) is brought to an end, and the assets and property of the company redistributed. _____ can also be referred to as winding-up or dissolution, although dissolution technically refers to the last stage of _____. The process of _____ also arises when customs, an authority or agency in a country responsible for collecting and safeguarding customs duties, determines the final computation or ascertainment of the duties or drawback accruing on an entry.
    a. BMC Software, Inc.
    b. 3M Company
    c. Bankruptcy protection
    d. Liquidation

4. In business and accounting, _____ are everything of value that is owned by a person or company. It is a claim on the property your income of a borrower. The balance sheet of a firm records the monetary value of the _____ owned by the firm.
    a. Earnings before interest, taxes, depreciation and amortization
    b. Accrual basis accounting
    c. Accounts receivable
    d. Assets

5. A _____ is a one-time payment of money, as opposed to a series of payments made over time.
    a. Manufacturing operations
    b. Trade name
    c. Lump sum
    d. Redemption value

6. _____ is generally understood in financial circles as the point at which revenue is recognized, typically through a transaction which involves the exchange of an asset, product, or service for cash or its equivalents.

This approach gives the accounting division a strictly objective basis for changing the books. For example, a homeowner may believe that his house has grown in value during a strong market, or fallen in value during a weak market, but until the house is actually sold for a specific price to a specific buyer, the change in value can only be estimated and is considered unrealized.

Chapter 16. Partnerships: Liquidation

a. Merck ' Co., Inc.
c. Valuation
b. Total-factor productivity
d. Realization

7. In accounting, _____ has a very specific meaning. It is an outflow of cash or other valuable assets from a person or company to another person or company. This outflow of cash is generally one side of a trade for products or services that have equal or better current or future value to the buyer than to the seller.
   a. ABC Television Network
   b. AMEX
   c. Expense
   d. AIG

8. A _____ is the transfer of wealth from one party (such as a person or company) to another. A _____ is usually made in exchange for the provision of goods, services or both, or to fulfill a legal obligation.

The simplest and oldest form of _____ is barter, the exchange of one good or service for another.

   a. BMC Software, Inc.
   b. Payee
   c. 3M Company
   d. Payment

9. _____ are formal records of a business' financial activities.

In British English, including United Kingdom company law, _____ are often referred to as accounts, although the term _____ is also used, particularly by accountants.

_____ provide an overview of a business' financial condition in both short and long term.

   a. Statement of retained earnings
   b. 3M Company
   c. Notes to the financial statements
   d. Financial Statements

10. In business, _____ is the total assets minus total outside liabilities of an individual or a company. For a company, this is called shareholders' equity and may be referred to as book value. _____ is stated as at a particular point in time.
    a. Restructuring
    b. Debtor
    c. Creditor
    d. Net worth

Chapter 17. Governmental Entities: Introduction and General Fund Accounting

1. _____ is an umbrella term which refers to the various accounting systems used by various public sector entities. In the United States, for instance, there are two levels of government which follow different accounting standards set forth by independent, private sector boards. At the federal level, the Federal Accounting Standards Advisory Board (FASAB) sets forth the accounting standards to follow.
   - a. Product control
   - b. Management accounting
   - c. Nonassurance services
   - d. Governmental accounting

2. In economics, _____ or _____ goods or real _____ refers to factors of production used to create goods or services that are not themselves significantly consumed (though they may depreciate) in the production process. _____ goods may be acquired with money or financial _____. In finance and accounting, _____ generally refers to financial wealth, especially that used to start or maintain a business.
   - a. Disclosure
   - b. Screening
   - c. Vyborg Appeal
   - d. Capital

3. The _____ is the national, professional association of CPAs in the United States, with more than 330,000 members, including CPAs in business and industry, public practice, government, and education; student affiliates; and international associates. It sets ethical standards for the profession and U.S. auditing standards for audits of private companies; federal, state and local governments; and non-profit organizations.

   Approximately 40% of its members are engaged in the practice of public accounting, in areas such as auditing, accounting, taxation, general business consulting, business valuation, personal financial planning and business technology.
   - a. American Institute of Certified Public Accountants
   - b. ABC Television Network
   - c. AIG
   - d. Other postemployment benefits

4. The general definition of an _____ is an evaluation of a person, organization, system, process, project or product. _____s are performed to ascertain the validity and reliability of information; also to provide an assessment of a system's internal control. The goal of an _____ is to express an opinion on the person/organization/system (etc) in question, under evaluation based on work done on a test basis.
   - a. Audit
   - b. Institute of Chartered Accountants of India
   - c. Assurance service
   - d. Audit regime

5. _____ is a term used in various fields. It often refers to an almanac or other compilation of statistics and information. The Tennessee _____ traces the term to the large blue velvet-covered books used for record-keeping by the Parliament of the United Kingdom beginning in the 15th century.
   - a. Help desk and incident reporting auditing
   - b. Starving the beast
   - c. Valuation
   - d. Blue book

6. The _____ is currently the source of generally accepted accounting principles (GAAP) used by State and Local governments in the [[United States of America]]. As with most of the entities involved in creating GAAP in the United States, it is a private, non-governmental organization.

   The _____ is subject to oversight by the Financial Accounting Foundation (FAF), which selects the members of the _____ and the Financial Accounting Standards Board, and funds both organizations.

Chapter 17. Governmental Entities: Introduction and General Fund Accounting

a. Fannie Mae
b. Multinational corporation
c. National Conference of Commissioners on Uniform State Laws
d. Governmental Accounting Standards Board

7. GASB stands for Governmental Accounting Standards Board. In June 1999, GASB Statement 34 (or _____) was published. _____ requires state and local governments to begin reporting all financial transactions, including the value of their infrastructure assets, roads, bridges, water and sewer facilities, and dams, in their annual financial reports on an accrual accounting basis.
   a. BMC Software, Inc.
   b. 3M Company
   c. BNSF Railway
   d. GASB 34

8. A municipality is an administrative entity composed of a clearly defined territory and its population and commonly denotes a city, town or a small grouping of them. A municipality is typically governed by a mayor and a city council or _____ council.

The notion of municipality includes townships but is not restricted to them.

   a. BNSF Railway
   b. 3M Company
   c. BMC Software, Inc.
   d. Municipal

9. The _____ duty is a legal relationship of confidence or trust between two or more parties, most commonly a _____ or trustee and a principal or beneficiary. One party, for example a corporate trust company or the trust department of a bank, holds a _____ relation or acts in a _____ capacity to another, such as one whose funds are entrusted to it for investment. In a _____ relation one person justifiably reposes confidence, good faith, reliance and trust in another whose aid, advice or protection is sought in some matter.
   a. Robinson-Patman Act
   b. FCPA
   c. Fiduciary
   d. Staple right

10. The word _____ indicates that a party, or proprietor, exercises private ownership, control or use over an item of property
    a. BMC Software, Inc.
    b. BNSF Railway
    c. 3M Company
    d. Proprietary

11. _____ is the term used in the United States to designate a unique charge government units can assess against real estate parcels for certain public projects. This charge is levied in a specific geographic area known as a _____ District (S.A.D.). A _____ may only be levied against parcels of real estate which have been identified as having received a direct and unique 'benefit' from the public project.Kadzban v City of Grandville, 502 N.W.2d 299, 501; Davies v City of Lawrence, 218 Kan.
    a. Special Assessment
    b. Malcolm Baldrige National Quality Award
    c. Fixed tax
    d. Tax Analysts

Chapter 17. Governmental Entities: Introduction and General Fund Accounting 89

12. In monetary economics _____ can refer either to a particular _____, for example British Pounds or United States Dollars, or, to the coins and banknotes of a particular _____, which actually form only a small part of the monetary base of a nation's money supply. The other part of a nation's money supply consists of money deposited in banks (sometimes called deposit money), ownership of which can be transferred by means of checks (cheques in the United Kingdom and Australia) or other forms of money transfer such as credit and debit cards. Deposit money and _____ are 'money' in the sense that both are acceptable as a means of exchange, but money need not necessarily be '_____'.

    a. BMC Software, Inc.
    b. BNSF Railway
    c. 3M Company
    d. Currency

13. _____ are formal records of a business' financial activities.

In British English, including United Kingdom company law, _____ are often referred to as accounts, although the term _____ is also used, particularly by accountants.

_____ provide an overview of a business' financial condition in both short and long term.

    a. Notes to the financial statements
    b. 3M Company
    c. Financial statements
    d. Statement of retained earnings

14. In financial accounting, a _____ or statement of financial position is a summary of a person's or organization's balances. Assets, liabilities and ownership equity are listed as of a specific date, such as the end of its financial year. A _____ is often described as a snapshot of a company's financial condition.

    a. Balance sheet
    b. 3M Company
    c. Financial statements
    d. Statement of retained earnings

15. _____ principle is a cornerstone of accrual accounting together with matching principle. They both determine the accounting period, in which revenues and expenses are recognized. According to the principle, revenues are recognized when they are (1) realized or realizable, and are (2) earned (usually when goods are transferred or services rendered), no matter when cash is received.

    a. Net realizable value
    b. 3M Company
    c. BMC Software, Inc.
    d. Revenue recognition

16. _____ is a common law doctrine that operates to ensure that property is not left in limbo and ownerless. It originally referred to a number of situations where a legal interest in land was destroyed by operation of law, so that the ownership of the land reverted to the immediately superior feudal lord.

Most common-law jurisdictions have abolished the concept of feudal tenure of property, and so the concept of _____ has lost something of its meaning.

    a. Employee Retirement Income Security Act
    b. Escheat
    c. Issued shares
    d. Independent contractor

17. Project _____: The project _____ is a prediction of the costs associated with a particular company project. These costs include labor, materials, and other related expenses. The project _____ is often broken down into specific tasks, with task _____s assigned to each.

a. BNSF Railway
b. Budget
c. 3M Company
d. BMC Software, Inc.

18. In finance, the _____ between two currencies specifies how much one currency is worth in terms of the other. It is the value of a foreign nation's currency in terms of the home nation's currency. For example an _____ of 102 Japanese yen to the United States dollar means that JPY 102 is worth the same as USD 1.

a. AMEX
b. Exchange rate
c. ABC Television Network
d. AIG

19. An _____ is the annual budget of an activity stated in terms of Budget Classification Code, functional/subfunctional categories and cost accounts. It contains estimates of the total value of resources required for the performance of the operation including reimbursable work or services for others. It also includes estimates of workload in terms of total work units identified by cost accounts.

a. Inventory turnover ratio
b. Authorised capital
c. Operating budget
d. Internality

20. _____ is the planning process used to determine whether a firm's long term investments such as new machinery, replacement machinery, new plants, new products, and research development projects are worth pursuing. It is budget for major capital, or investment, expenditures.

Many formal methods are used in _____, including the techniques such as

- Net present value
- Profitability index
- Internal rate of return
- Modified Internal Rate of Return
- Equivalent annuity

These methods use the incremental cash flows from each potential investment, or project. Techniques based on accounting earnings and accounting rules are sometimes used - though economists consider this to be improper - such as the accounting rate of return, and 'return on investment.' Simplified and hybrid methods are used as well, such as payback period and discounted payback period.

a. Gross profit
b. Preferred stock
c. Cash flow
d. Capital budgeting

21. In business and accounting, _____ are everything of value that is owned by a person or company. It is a claim on the property your income of a borrower. The balance sheet of a firm records the monetary value of the _____ owned by the firm.

a. Assets
b. Accrual basis accounting
c. Accounts receivable
d. Earnings before interest, taxes, depreciation and amortization

22. _____ is a legal term of art for anything that affects or limits the title of a property, such as mortgages, leases, easements, liens, or restrictions. Also, those considered as potentially making the title defeasible are also _____s. For example, charging orders, building orders and structure alteration.

Chapter 17. Governmental Entities: Introduction and General Fund Accounting

a. Ownership
b. ABC Television Network
c. Encumbrance
d. Administrative proceeding

23. In financial accounting, a _____ is defined as an obligation of an entity arising from past transactions or events, the settlement of which may result in the transfer or use of assets, provision of services or other yielding of economic benefits in the future.
   a. Corporate governance
   b. Liability
   c. Vested
   d. False Claims Act

24. The term _____ refers to government debt, expenditures and revenues, or to finance (particularly financial revenue) in general.

- _____ deficit is the budget deficit of federal or local government
- _____ policy is the discretionary spending of governments. Contrasts with monetary policy.
- _____ year and _____ quarter are reporting periods for firms and other agencies.

See also

- Procurator _____ and Crown Office and Procurator _____ Service

a. Scientific Research and Experimental Development Tax Incentive Program
b. Fiscal
c. Swap
d. Comparable

25. _____ is the balance of the amounts of cash being received and paid by a business during a defined period of time, sometimes tied to a specific project. Measurement of _____ can be used

- to evaluate the state or performance of a business or project.
- to determine problems with liquidity. Being profitable does not necessarily mean being liquid. A company can fail because of a shortage of cash, even while profitable.
- to project rate of returns. The time of _____s into and out of projects are used as inputs to financial models such as internal rate of return, and net present value.
- to examine income or growth of a business when it is believed that accrual accounting concepts do not represent economic realities. Alternately, _____ can be used to 'validate' the net income generated by accrual accounting.

_____ as a generic term may be used differently depending on context, and certain _____ definitions may be adapted by analysts and users for their own uses. Common terms include operating _____ and free _____.

a. Controlling interest
b. Cash flow
c. Flow-through entity
d. Commercial paper

Chapter 17. Governmental Entities: Introduction and General Fund Accounting

26. A _____ is a hedge of the exposure to the variability of cash flow that

   1. is attributable to a particular risk associated with a recognized asset or liability. Such as all or some future interest payments on variable rate debt or a highly probable forecast transaction and
   2. could affect profit or loss

   a. 3M Company
   b. Currency risk
   c. Credit risk
   d. Cash flow hedge

27. _____ refers to a business or organization attempting to acquire goods or services to accomplish the goals of the enterprise. Though there are several organizations that attempt to set standards in the _____ process, processes can vary greatly between organizations. Typically the word e;_____e; is not used interchangeably with the word e;procuremente;, since procurement typically includes Expediting, Supplier Quality, and Traffic and Logistics (T'L) in addition to _____.

   a. Consignor
   b. Supply chain
   c. Purchasing
   d. Free port

28. _____ is a common concept in economics, and gives rise to derived concepts such as consumer debt. Generally _____ is defined by opposition to production. But the precise definition can vary because different schools of economists define production quite differently.

   a. Starving the beast
   b. Yield
   c. Mitigating Control
   d. Consumption

29. _____, also known as property, plant, and equipment (PP&E), is a term used in accountancy for assets and property which cannot easily be converted into cash. This can be compared with current assets such as cash or bank accounts, which are described as liquid assets. In most cases, only tangible assets are referred to as fixed.

   a. Bankruptcy prediction
   b. Subledger
   c. Minority interest
   d. Fixed asset

30. The _____ is the former authoritative body of the American Institute of Certified Public Accountants (AICPA.) It was created by the American Institute of Certified Public Accountants in 1959 and issued pronouncements on accounting principles until 1973, when it was replaced by the Financial Accounting Standards Board (FASB.)

   The _____ was disbanded in the hopes that the smaller, fully-independent FASB could more effectively create accounting standards.

   a. Institute of Management Accountants
   b. International Federation of Accountants
   c. American Payroll Association
   d. Accounting Principles Board

31. _____ is a type of lease - the other being an operating lease. A _____ effectively allows a firm to finance the purchase of an asset, even if, strictly speaking, the firm never acquires the asset. Typically, a _____ will give the lessee control over an asset for a large proportion of the asset's useful life, providing them the benefits and risks of ownership.

   a. Profitability index
   b. 3M Company
   c. Debt ratio
   d. Finance lease

Chapter 17. Governmental Entities: Introduction and General Fund Accounting

32. _____ is a form of corporation equity ownership represented in the securities. It is a stock whose dividends are based on market fluctuations. It is dangerous in comparison to preferred shares and some other investment options, in that in the event of bankruptcy, _____ investors receive their funds after preferred stock holders, bondholders, creditors, etc. On the other hand, common shares on average perform better than preferred shares or bonds over time.
   a. Common Stock
   b. Growth investing
   c. 3M Company
   d. Stock split

33. _____ in accounting is the process of treating equity investments, usually 20-50%, in associate companies. The investor keeps such equities as an asset. Proportional share of associate company's net income increases the investment, and proportional payment of dividends decreases it.
   a. AIG
   b. ABC Television Network
   c. Out-of-pocket
   d. Equity Method

34. A _____ is a contract conferring a right on one person to possess property belonging to another person (called a landlord or lessor) to the exclusion of the owner landlord. It is a rental agreement between landlord and tenant. The relationship between the tenant and the landlord is called a tenancy, and the right to possession by the tenant is sometimes called a leasehold interest.
   a. Lease
   b. Model Code of Professional Responsibility
   c. Federal Sentencing Guidelines
   d. Robinson-Patman Act

35. In economic models, the _____ time frame assumes no fixed factors of production. Firms can enter or leave the marketplace, and the cost (and availability) of land, labor, raw materials, and capital goods can be assumed to vary. In contrast, in the short-run time frame, certain factors are assumed to be fixed, because there is not sufficient time for them to change.
   a. Long-run
   b. Short-run
   c. BMC Software, Inc.
   d. 3M Company

36. _____ is that which is owed; usually referencing assets owed, but the term can also cover moral obligations and other interactions not requiring money. In the case of assets, _____ is a means of using future purchasing power in the present before a summation has been earned. Some companies and corporations use _____ as a part of their overall corporate finance strategy.
   a. Lender
   b. Loan
   c. Debt
   d. Debenture

37. A _____ is a type of debt Like all debt instruments, a _____ entails the redistribution of financial assets over time, between the lender and the borrower.
   a. Loan to value
   b. Debenture
   c. Lender
   d. Loan

38. A _____ is a party (e.g. person, organization, company, or government) that has a claim to the services of a second party. It is a person or institution to whom money is owed. The first party, in general, has provided some property or service to the second party under the assumption (usually enforced by contract) that the second party will return an equivalent property or service.
   a. Creditor
   b. Par value
   c. Treasury company
   d. Payback period

Chapter 17. Governmental Entities: Introduction and General Fund Accounting

39. _____ is any physical or virtual entity that is owned by an individual or jointly by a group of individuals. An owner of _____ has the right to consume, sell, rent, mortgage, transfer and exchange his or her _____. Important widely-recognized types of _____ include real _____, personal _____ (other physical possessions), and intellectual _____ (rights over artistic creations, inventions, etc.), although the latter is not always as widely recognized or enforced.

   a. Property
   b. Fiduciary
   c. Primary authority
   d. Disclosure requirement

40. _____ is revenue from peripheral (non-core) operations. For example, a company that manufactures and sells automobiles would record the revenue from the sale of an automobile as 'regular' revenue. If that same company also rented a portion of one of its buildings, it would record that revenue as e;_____e; and disclose it separately on its income statement to show that it is from something other than its core operations.

   a. AIG
   b. AMEX
   c. ABC Television Network
   d. Other revenue

41. The term _____ has three unrelated technical definitions, and is also used in a variety of non-technical ways.

- In financial economics, it refers to any asset used to make money, as opposed to assets used for personal enjoyment or consumption. This is an important distinction because two people can disagree sharply about the value of personal assets, one person might think a sports car is more valuable than a pickup truck, another person might have the opposite taste. But if an asset is held for the purpose of making money, taste has nothing to do with it, only differences of opinion about how much money the asset will produce. With the further assumption that people agree on the probability distribution of future cash flows, it is possible to have an objective _____ pricing model. Even without the assumption of agreement, it is possible to set rational limits on _____ value.
- In governmental accounting, it is defined as any asset used in operations with an initial useful life extending beyond one reporting period. Generally, government managers have a 'stewardship' duty to maintain _____s under their control. See International Public Sector Accounting Standards for details.
- In US tax accounting, it is defined as any property other than a list of exceptions. The main exceptions are anything held for sale, and any real estate or depreciable property used in business. Almost everything you own and use for personal purposes, pleasure or investment is a _____. If something is a _____ for tax purposes, gains or losses on sale or disposition are capital gains or capital losses. For individuals, however, capital losses on property held for personal use are generally not deductible. See the IRS publication Tax Facts about Capital Gains and Losses for details.

A well-known financial accounting textbook advises that the term be avoided except in tax accounting because it is used in so many different senses, not all of them well-defined. For example it is often used as a synonym for fixed assets or for investments in securities.

A common non-technical usage occurs when people ask that employees or the environment or something else be treated as a _____.

   a. Solvency
   b. Capital asset
   c. BMC Software, Inc.
   d. 3M Company

Chapter 17. Governmental Entities: Introduction and General Fund Accounting 95

42. An _____ is the buying of one company by another. An _____ may be friendly or hostile. In the former case, the companies cooperate in negotiations; in the latter case, the takeover target is unwilling to be bought or the target's board has no prior knowledge of the offer. _____ usually refers to a purchase of a smaller firm by a larger one. Sometimes, however, a smaller firm will acquire management control of a larger or longer established company and keep its name for the combined entity. This is known as a reverse takeover.
   a. AMEX
   b. Acquisition
   c. ABC Television Network
   d. AIG

43. In accounting/accountancy, _____ are journal entries usually made at the end of an accounting period to allocate income and expenditure to the period in which they actually occurred. The revenue recognition principle is the basis of making _____ that pertain to unearned and accrued revenues under accrual-basis accounting. They are sometimes called Balance Day adjustments because they are made on balance day.
   a. Accrued expense
   b. Earnings before interest, taxes, depreciation and amortization
   c. Accrual
   d. Adjusting entries

44. _____ are journal entries made at the end of an accounting period to transfer temporary accounts to permanent accounts. An 'income summary' account may be used to show the balance between revenue and expenses, or they could be directly closed against retained earnings where dividend payments will be deducted from. This process is used to reset the balance of these temporary accounts to zero for the next accounting period.
   a. Treasury stock
   b. Trial balance
   c. Closing entries
   d. FIFO and LIFO accounting

Chapter 18. Governmental Entities: Special Funds and Government-wide Financial Statements

1. _____ is an umbrella term which refers to the various accounting systems used by various public sector entities. In the United States, for instance, there are two levels of government which follow different accounting standards set forth by independent, private sector boards. At the federal level, the Federal Accounting Standards Advisory Board (FASAB) sets forth the accounting standards to follow.

   a. Product control
   b. Governmental accounting
   c. Management accounting
   d. Nonassurance services

2. The _____ is currently the source of generally accepted accounting principles (GAAP) used by State and Local governments in the [[United States of America]]. As with most of the entities involved in creating GAAP in the United States, it is a private, non-governmental organization.

   The _____ is subject to oversight by the Financial Accounting Foundation (FAF), which selects the members of the _____ and the Financial Accounting Standards Board, and funds both organizations.

   a. Fannie Mae
   b. Governmental Accounting Standards Board
   c. National Conference of Commissioners on Uniform State Laws
   d. Multinational corporation

3. In economics, _____ or _____ goods or real _____ refers to factors of production used to create goods or services that are not themselves significantly consumed (though they may depreciate) in the production process. _____ goods may be acquired with money or financial _____. In finance and accounting, _____ generally refers to financial wealth, especially that used to start or maintain a business.

   a. Capital
   b. Vyborg Appeal
   c. Screening
   d. Disclosure

4. _____ are formal records of a business' financial activities.

   In British English, including United Kingdom company law, _____ are often referred to as accounts, although the term _____ is also used, particularly by accountants.

   _____ provide an overview of a business' financial condition in both short and long term.

   a. Statement of retained earnings
   b. 3M Company
   c. Notes to the financial statements
   d. Financial statements

5. _____ are financial statements that factor the holding company's subsidiaries into its aggregated accounting figure. It is a representation of how the holding company is doing as a group. The consolidated accounts should provide a true and fair view of the financial and operating conditions of the group.

   a. Redemption value
   b. Replacement cost
   c. Committee on Accounting Procedure
   d. Consolidated financial statements

6. A _____ is a piece of paper, often preprinted in a way designed to help organize material for learning or clear understanding. Students in a school may have 'fill-in-the-blank' sheets of questions, diagrams or maps to help them with their exercises. Students will often use _____s to review what has been taught in class.

   a. 3M Company
   b. Value based pricing
   c. BMC Software, Inc.
   d. Worksheet

Chapter 18. Governmental Entities: Special Funds and Government-wide Financial Statements

7. In finance, a _____ is a debt security, in which the authorized issuer owes the holders a debt and, depending on the terms of the _____, is obliged to pay interest (the coupon) and/or to repay the principal at a later date, termed maturity. It is a formal contract to repay borrowed money with interest at fixed intervals.

Thus a _____ is like a loan: the issuer is the borrower, the _____ holder is the lender, and the coupon is the interest.

a. Coupon rate
b. Zero-coupon bond
c. Revenue bonds
d. Bond

8. _____ are journal entries made at the end of an accounting period to transfer temporary accounts to permanent accounts. An 'income summary' account may be used to show the balance between revenue and expenses, or they could be directly closed against retained earnings where dividend payments will be deducted from. This process is used to reset the balance of these temporary accounts to zero for the next accounting period.

a. FIFO and LIFO accounting
b. Trial balance
c. Treasury stock
d. Closing entries

9. _____ is a type of lease - the other being an operating lease. A _____ effectively allows a firm to finance the purchase of an asset, even if, strictly speaking, the firm never acquires the asset. Typically, a _____ will give the lessee control over an asset for a large proportion of the asset's useful life, providing them the benefits and risks of ownership.

a. Debt ratio
b. Profitability index
c. 3M Company
d. Finance lease

10. _____ is that which is owed; usually referencing assets owed, but the term can also cover moral obligations and other interactions not requiring money. In the case of assets, _____ is a means of using future purchasing power in the present before a summation has been earned. Some companies and corporations use _____ as a part of their overall corporate finance strategy.

a. Debenture
b. Lender
c. Loan
d. Debt

11. _____ are financial bonds that mature in installments over a period of time. In effect, a $100,000, 5-year serial bond would mature in a $20,000 annuity over a 5-year interval. Bond issues consisting of a series of blocks of securities maturing in sequence, the coupon rate can be different.

a. Serial bonds
b. Household and Dependent Care Credit
c. Just-in-time
d. Low Income Housing Tax Credit

12. _____ is the term used in the United States to designate a unique charge government units can assess against real estate parcels for certain public projects. This charge is levied in a specific geographic area known as a _____ District (S.A.D.). A _____ may only be levied against parcels of real estate which have been identified as having received a direct and unique 'benefit' from the public project.Kadzban v City of Grandville, 502 N.W.2d 299, 501; Davies v City of Lawrence, 218 Kan.

a. Special assessment
b. Fixed tax
c. Malcolm Baldrige National Quality Award
d. Tax Analysts

Chapter 18. Governmental Entities: Special Funds and Government-wide Financial Statements

13. A _____ is a contract conferring a right on one person to possess property belonging to another person (called a landlord or lessor) to the exclusion of the owner landlord. It is a rental agreement between landlord and tenant. The relationship between the tenant and the landlord is called a tenancy, and the right to possession by the tenant is sometimes called a leasehold interest.
    a. Federal Sentencing Guidelines
    b. Model Code of Professional Responsibility
    c. Robinson-Patman Act
    d. Lease

14. Project _____: The project _____ is a prediction of the costs associated with a particular company project. These costs include labor, materials, and other related expenses. The project _____ is often broken down into specific tasks, with task _____s assigned to each.
    a. BMC Software, Inc.
    b. 3M Company
    c. BNSF Railway
    d. Budget

15. _____ is a fee paid on borrowed assets. It is the price paid for the use of borrowed money, or, money earned by deposited funds. Assets that are sometimes lent with _____ include money, shares, consumer goods through hire purchase, major assets such as aircraft, and even entire factories in finance lease arrangements. The _____ is calculated upon the value of the assets in the same manner as upon money.
    a. Interest
    b. Insolvency
    c. AIG
    d. ABC Television Network

16. GASB stands for Governmental Accounting Standards Board. In June 1999, GASB Statement 34 (or _____) was published. _____ requires state and local governments to begin reporting all financial transactions, including the value of their infrastructure assets, roads, bridges, water and sewer facilities, and dams, in their annual financial reports on an accrual accounting basis.
    a. BNSF Railway
    b. 3M Company
    c. BMC Software, Inc.
    d. GASB 34

17. An _____ is the buying of one company by another. An _____ may be friendly or hostile. In the former case, the companies cooperate in negotiations; in the latter case, the takeover target is unwilling to be bought or the target's board has no prior knowledge of the offer. _____ usually refers to a purchase of a smaller firm by a larger one. Sometimes, however, a smaller firm will acquire management control of a larger or longer established company and keep its name for the combined entity. This is known as a reverse takeover.
    a. AIG
    b. ABC Television Network
    c. AMEX
    d. Acquisition

18. In business and accounting, _____ are everything of value that is owned by a person or company. It is a claim on the property your income of a borrower. The balance sheet of a firm records the monetary value of the _____ owned by the firm.
    a. Earnings before interest, taxes, depreciation and amortization
    b. Accounts receivable
    c. Accrual basis accounting
    d. Assets

Chapter 18. Governmental Entities: Special Funds and Government-wide Financial Statements

19. The term _____ has three unrelated technical definitions, and is also used in a variety of non-technical ways.

- In financial economics, it refers to any asset used to make money, as opposed to assets used for personal enjoyment or consumption. This is an important distinction because two people can disagree sharply about the value of personal assets, one person might think a sports car is more valuable than a pickup truck, another person might have the opposite taste. But if an asset is held for the purpose of making money, taste has nothing to do with it, only differences of opinion about how much money the asset will produce. With the further assumption that people agree on the probability distribution of future cash flows, it is possible to have an objective _____ pricing model. Even without the assumption of agreement, it is possible to set rational limits on _____ value.
- In governmental accounting, it is defined as any asset used in operations with an initial useful life extending beyond one reporting period. Generally, government managers have a 'stewardship' duty to maintain _____s under their control. See International Public Sector Accounting Standards for details.
- In US tax accounting, it is defined as any property other than a list of exceptions. The main exceptions are anything held for sale, and any real estate or depreciable property used in business. Almost everything you own and use for personal purposes, pleasure or investment is a _____. If something is a _____ for tax purposes, gains or losses on sale or disposition are capital gains or capital losses. For individuals, however, capital losses on property held for personal use are generally not deductible. See the IRS publication Tax Facts about Capital Gains and Losses for details.

A well-known financial accounting textbook advises that the term be avoided except in tax accounting because it is used in so many different senses, not all of them well-defined. For example it is often used as a synonym for fixed assets or for investments in securities.

A common non-technical usage occurs when people ask that employees or the environment or something else be treated as a _____.

a. Capital asset
b. Solvency
c. BMC Software, Inc.
d. 3M Company

20. In accounting, _____ has a very specific meaning. It is an outflow of cash or other valuable assets from a person or company to another person or company. This outflow of cash is generally one side of a trade for products or services that have equal or better current or future value to the buyer than to the seller.

a. AIG
b. ABC Television Network
c. AMEX
d. Expense

21. The word _____ indicates that a party, or proprietor, exercises private ownership, control or use over an item of property

a. BNSF Railway
b. BMC Software, Inc.
c. 3M Company
d. Proprietary

Chapter 18. Governmental Entities: Special Funds and Government-wide Financial Statements

22. _____ is the balance of the amounts of cash being received and paid by a business during a defined period of time, sometimes tied to a specific project. Measurement of _____ can be used

- to evaluate the state or performance of a business or project.
- to determine problems with liquidity. Being profitable does not necessarily mean being liquid. A company can fail because of a shortage of cash, even while profitable.
- to project rate of returns. The time of _____s into and out of projects are used as inputs to financial models such as internal rate of return, and net present value.
- to examine income or growth of a business when it is believed that accrual accounting concepts do not represent economic realities. Alternately, _____ can be used to 'validate' the net income generated by accrual accounting.

_____ as a generic term may be used differently depending on context, and certain _____ definitions may be adapted by analysts and users for their own uses. Common terms include operating _____ and free _____.

a. Commercial paper
b. Controlling interest
c. Flow-through entity
d. Cash Flow

23. _____ is an accounting system often used by nonprofit organizations and by the public sector. According to StartHereGoPlaces, _____ is a '[m]ethod of accounting and presentation whereby assets and liabilities are grouped according to the purpose for which they are to be used.'

_____ serves any nonprofit organization or the public sector. These organizations have a need for special reporting to financial statements users that show how money is spent, rather than how much profit was earned.

a. Liquidating dividend
b. Fund Accounting
c. Refunding
d. Replacement cost

24. An _____ is a term used in behavioral economics to describe those types of behaviors that impose costs on a person in the long-run that are not taken into account when making decisions in the present. Classical Economics discourages government from creating legislation that targets internalities, because it is assumed that the consumer takes these personal costs into account when paying for the good that causes the _____. For example, cigarettes should be taxed because of the negative consumption externalities that they impose, such as second-hand smoke, not because the smoker harms him or herself by smoking.

a. Authorised capital
b. Operating budget
c. Inventory turnover ratio
d. Internality

25. In monetary economics _____ can refer either to a particular _____, for example British Pounds or United States Dollars, or, to the coins and banknotes of a particular _____, which actually form only a small part of the monetary base of a nation's money supply. The other part of a nation's money supply consists of money deposited in banks (sometimes called deposit money), ownership of which can be transferred by means of checks (cheques in the United Kingdom and Australia) or other forms of money transfer such as credit and debit cards. Deposit money and _____ are 'money' in the sense that both are acceptable as a means of exchange, but money need not necessarily be '_____'.

a. Currency
b. 3M Company
c. BMC Software, Inc.
d. BNSF Railway

Chapter 18. Governmental Entities: Special Funds and Government-wide Financial Statements

26. _____, also known as property, plant, and equipment (PP&E), is a term used in accountancy for assets and property which cannot easily be converted into cash. This can be compared with current assets such as cash or bank accounts, which are described as liquid assets. In most cases, only tangible assets are referred to as fixed.
   a. Minority interest
   b. Subledger
   c. Bankruptcy prediction
   d. Fixed asset

27. _____ are annual financial statements or reports for the year. The financial statements, in contrast to budget, present the revenue collected and amounts spent. The _____ usually include a statement of activities (similar to an income statement in the private sector), a balance sheet and often some type of reconciliation.
   a. Government financial statements
   b. 3M Company
   c. BNSF Railway
   d. BMC Software, Inc.

28. _____ means the giving out of information, either voluntarily or to be in compliance with legal regulations or workplace rules.

   - In Computer security, full _____ means disclosing full information about vulnerabilities.
   - In computing, _____ widget
   - Journalism, full _____ refers to disclosing the interests of the writer which may bear on the subject being written about, for example, if the writer has worked with an interview subject in the past.

   - In law:
     - The law of England and Wales, _____ refers to a process that may form part of legal proceedings, whereby parties inform to other parties the existence of any relevant documents that are, or have been, in their control. This compares with the process known as discovery in the course of legal proceedings in the United States.
     - In U.S. civil procedure (litigation rules for civil cases), _____ is a stage prior to trial. In civil cases, each party must disclose to the opposing party the following: names of witnesses which it may use to support its side, copies of documents (or mere description of these documents) in its control which it may use to support its side, computation of damages claimed, and certain insurance information. _____ is related to, but technically prior to, the discovery stage.
     - In Company law (known as 'corporate law' in the United States), _____ refers to giving out information about public or limited companies or their officers, which might be kept secret if the company was a private company or a partnership.

   - In real property transactions, _____ refers to providing to a buyer information known to the seller or broker/agent concerning the condition or other aspects of real property that would affect the property's value or desirability. These rules regarding what information must be disclosed, and whether the information must be disclosed even if a buyer does not ask, vary from one jurisdiction to the next.

   a. Tax harmonisation
   b. Controlled Foreign Corporations
   c. Trailing
   d. Disclosure

29. Employment is a contract between two parties, one being the employer and the other being the _____. An _____ may be defined as: 'A person in the service of another under any contract of hire, express or implied, oral or written, where the employer has the power or right to control and direct the _____ in the material details of how the work is to be performed.' Black's Law Dictionary page 471 (5th ed. 1979).

a. AIG
b. Employee
c. AMEX
d. ABC Television Network

30. In economics, a _____ is a type of pension plan in which an employer promises a specified monthly benefit on retirement that is predetermined by a formula based on the employee's earnings history, tenure of service and age, rather than depending on investment returns. It is 'defined' in the sense that the formula for computing the employer's contribution is known in advance. In the United States, 26 U.S.C.

a. BMC Software, Inc.
b. Fixed asset turnover
c. 3M Company
d. Defined Benefit Pension Plan

31. The term _____ or superannuation refers to a pension granted upon retirement. They may be set up by employers, insurance companies, the government or other institutions such as employer associations or trade unions.

a. 3M Company
b. BMC Software, Inc.
c. Retirement plan
d. Wage

Chapter 19. Not-for-Profit Entities

1. The _____ is a private, not-for-profit organization whose primary purpose is to develop generally accepted accounting principles (GAAP) within the United States in the public's interest. The Securities and Exchange Commission (SEC) designated the _____ as the organization responsible for setting accounting standards for public companies in the U.S. It was created in 1973, replacing the Accounting Principles Board and the Committee on Accounting Procedure of the American Institute of Certified Public Accountants. The _____'s mission is 'to establish and improve standards of financial accounting and reporting for the guidance and education of the public, including issuers, auditors, and users of financial information.'

The _____ is not a governmental body.

a. Governmental Accounting Standards Board
b. Public company
c. Fannie Mae
d. Financial Accounting Standards Board

2. _____ are formal records of a business' financial activities.

In British English, including United Kingdom company law, _____ are often referred to as accounts, although the term _____ is also used, particularly by accountants.

_____ provide an overview of a business' financial condition in both short and long term.

a. 3M Company
b. Notes to the financial statements
c. Statement of retained earnings
d. Financial Statements

3. In business and accounting, _____ are everything of value that is owned by a person or company. It is a claim on the property your income of a borrower. The balance sheet of a firm records the monetary value of the _____ owned by the firm.

a. Accounts receivable
b. Earnings before interest, taxes, depreciation and amortization
c. Accrual basis accounting
d. Assets

4. _____ is a term used in accounting, economics and finance to spread the cost of an asset over the span of several years.

In simple words we can say that _____ is the reduction in the value of an asset due to usage, passage of time, wear and tear, technological outdating or obsolescence, depletion, inadequacy, rot, rust, decay or other such factors.

In accounting, _____ is a term used to describe any method of attributing the historical or purchase cost of an asset across its useful life, roughly corresponding to normal wear and tear.

a. Net profit
b. General ledger
c. Current asset
d. Depreciation

5. _____ principle is a cornerstone of accrual accounting together with matching principle. They both determine the accounting period, in which revenues and expenses are recognized. According to the principle, revenues are recognized when they are (1) realized or realizable, and are (2) earned (usually when goods are transferred or services rendered), no matter when cash is received.

Chapter 19. Not-for-Profit Entities

a. BMC Software, Inc.
c. 3M Company
b. Net realizable value
d. Revenue recognition

6. The _____ is currently the source of generally accepted accounting principles (GAAP) used by State and Local governments in the [[United States of America]]. As with most of the entities involved in creating GAAP in the United States, it is a private, non-governmental organization.

The _____ is subject to oversight by the Financial Accounting Foundation (FAF), which selects the members of the _____ and the Financial Accounting Standards Board, and funds both organizations.

a. Fannie Mae
c. National Conference of Commissioners on Uniform State Laws
b. Multinational corporation
d. Governmental Accounting Standards Board

7. GASB stands for Governmental Accounting Standards Board. In June 1999, GASB Statement 34 (or _____) was published. _____ requires state and local governments to begin reporting all financial transactions, including the value of their infrastructure assets, roads, bridges, water and sewer facilities, and dams, in their annual financial reports on an accrual accounting basis.

a. BMC Software, Inc.
c. BNSF Railway
b. GASB 34
d. 3M Company

8. The _____ (HFMA) is a non-profit membership organization for healthcare financial management executives. The organization is based in Westchester, Chicago, Illinois. Founded on September 30, 1946, _____ serves over 35,000 members, which include CFOs, controllers, and accountants.

a. MicroStrategy
c. Privately held
b. Freddie Mac
d. HFMA

9. In financial accounting, a _____ or statement of financial position is a summary of a person's or organization's balances. Assets, liabilities and ownership equity are listed as of a specific date, such as the end of its financial year. A _____ is often described as a snapshot of a company's financial condition.

a. 3M Company
c. Statement of retained earnings
b. Financial statements
d. Balance sheet

10. The _____ is the former authoritative body of the American Institute of Certified Public Accountants (AICPA.) It was created by the American Institute of Certified Public Accountants in 1959 and issued pronouncements on accounting principles until 1973, when it was replaced by the Financial Accounting Standards Board (FASB.)

The _____ was disbanded in the hopes that the smaller, fully-independent FASB could more effectively create accounting standards.

a. Accounting Principles Board
c. American Payroll Association
b. Institute of Management Accountants
d. International Federation of Accountants

Chapter 19. Not-for-Profit Entities

11. _____ is a form of corporation equity ownership represented in the securities. It is a stock whose dividends are based on market fluctuations. It is dangerous in comparison to preferred shares and some other investment options, in that in the event of bankruptcy, _____ investors receive their funds after preferred stock holders, bondholders, creditors, etc. On the other hand, common shares on average perform better than preferred shares or bonds over time.
    a. 3M Company
    b. Stock split
    c. Common Stock
    d. Growth investing

12. _____ is that which is owed; usually referencing assets owed, but the term can also cover moral obligations and other interactions not requiring money. In the case of assets, _____ is a means of using future purchasing power in the present before a summation has been earned. Some companies and corporations use _____ as a part of their overall corporate finance strategy.
    a. Debt
    b. Debenture
    c. Loan
    d. Lender

13. _____ in accounting is the process of treating equity investments, usually 20-50%, in associate companies. The investor keeps such equities as an asset. Proportional share of associate company's net income increases the investment, and proportional payment of dividends decreases it.
    a. ABC Television Network
    b. Equity Method
    c. AIG
    d. Out-of-pocket

14. A _____ is a fungible, negotiable instrument representing financial value. they are broadly categorized into debt securities (such as banknotes, bonds and debentures), and equity securities; e.g., common stocks. The company or other entity issuing the _____ is called the issuer.
    a. 3M Company
    b. Tracking stock
    c. BMC Software, Inc.
    d. Security

15. _____ is an umbrella term which refers to the various accounting systems used by various public sector entities. In the United States, for instance, there are two levels of government which follow different accounting standards set forth by independent, private sector boards. At the federal level, the Federal Accounting Standards Advisory Board (FASAB) sets forth the accounting standards to follow.
    a. Nonassurance services
    b. Governmental accounting
    c. Product control
    d. Management accounting

16. In economic models, the _____ time frame assumes no fixed factors of production. Firms can enter or leave the marketplace, and the cost (and availability) of land, labor, raw materials, and capital goods can be assumed to vary. In contrast, in the short-run time frame, certain factors are assumed to be fixed, because there is not sufficient time for them to change.
    a. BMC Software, Inc.
    b. 3M Company
    c. Short-run
    d. Long-run

17. _____ are sometimes the same as net worth, or shareholders' equity - assets minus liabilities. The term _____ is commonly used with charities or not for profit entities. Although these entities don't make money, it is important to maintain reasonable reserves to help future growth.
    a. Net interest spread
    b. Sortino ratio
    c. Debtor days
    d. Net assets

Chapter 19. Not-for-Profit Entities

18. In financial accounting, a _____ or Statement of cash flows is a financial statement that shows a company's flow of cash. The money coming into the business is called cash inflow, and money going out from the business is called cash outflow. The statement shows how changes in balance sheet and income accounts affect cash and cash equivalents, and breaks the analysis down to operating, investing, and financing activities.
    a. Cash flow statement
    b. BMC Software, Inc.
    c. BNSF Railway
    d. 3M Company

19. _____ is the balance of the amounts of cash being received and paid by a business during a defined period of time, sometimes tied to a specific project. Measurement of _____ can be used

    - to evaluate the state or performance of a business or project.
    - to determine problems with liquidity. Being profitable does not necessarily mean being liquid. A company can fail because of a shortage of cash, even while profitable.
    - to project rate of returns. The time of _____s into and out of projects are used as inputs to financial models such as internal rate of return, and net present value.
    - to examine income or growth of a business when it is believed that accrual accounting concepts do not represent economic realities. Alternately, _____ can be used to 'validate' the net income generated by accrual accounting.

    _____ as a generic term may be used differently depending on context, and certain _____ definitions may be adapted by analysts and users for their own uses. Common terms include operating _____ and free _____.

    a. Flow-through entity
    b. Controlling interest
    c. Commercial paper
    d. Cash flow

20. An _____, operating expenditure, operational expense, operational expenditure or OPEX is an on-going cost for running a product, business, or system. Its counterpart, a capital expenditure (CAPEX), is the cost of developing or providing non-consumable parts for the product or system. For example, the purchase of a photocopier is the CAPEX, and the annual paper and toner cost is the OPEX.
    a. AMEX
    b. AIG
    c. ABC Television Network
    d. Operating expense

21. In accounting, _____ has a very specific meaning. It is an outflow of cash or other valuable assets from a person or company to another person or company. This outflow of cash is generally one side of a trade for products or services that have equal or better current or future value to the buyer than to the seller.
    a. AMEX
    b. AIG
    c. ABC Television Network
    d. Expense

22. The general definition of an _____ is an evaluation of a person, organization, system, process, project or product. _____s are performed to ascertain the validity and reliability of information; also to provide an assessment of a system's internal control. The goal of an _____ is to express an opinion on the person/organization/system (etc) in question, under evaluation based on work done on a test basis.
    a. Audit regime
    b. Institute of Chartered Accountants of India
    c. Assurance service
    d. Audit

Chapter 19. Not-for-Profit Entities

23. _____ is financial assistance paid to people by governments. Some _____ is general, while specific and can only be invoked under certain circumstances, such as a scholarship. _____ payments can be made to individuals or to companies or entities--these latter payments are often considered corporate _____.
    a. Swap
    b. Joseph Ronald Banister
    c. Price-to-sales ratio
    d. Welfare

24. In monetary economics _____ can refer either to a particular _____, for example British Pounds or United States Dollars, or, to the coins and banknotes of a particular _____, which actually form only a small part of the monetary base of a nation's money supply. The other part of a nation's money supply consists of money deposited in banks (sometimes called deposit money), ownership of which can be transferred by means of checks (cheques in the United Kingdom and Australia) or other forms of money transfer such as credit and debit cards. Deposit money and _____ are 'money' in the sense that both are acceptable as a means of exchange, but money need not necessarily be '_____'.
    a. Currency
    b. BNSF Railway
    c. 3M Company
    d. BMC Software, Inc.

25. In economics, business, retail, and accounting, a _____ is the value of money that has been used up to produce something, and hence is not available for use anymore. In economics, a _____ is an alternative that is given up as a result of a decision. In business, the _____ may be one of acquisition, in which case the amount of money expended to acquire it is counted as _____.
    a. Cost allocation
    b. Prime cost
    c. Cost of quality
    d. Cost

26. In accounting, _____ or carrying value is the value of an asset according to its balance sheet account balance. For assets, the value is based on the original cost of the asset less any depreciation, amortization or impairment costs made against the asset. Traditionally, a company's _____ is its total assets minus intangible assets and liabilities.
    a. Depreciation
    b. Matching principle
    c. Generally accepted accounting principles
    d. Book value

Chapter 20. Corporations in Financial Difficulty

1. _____ means the inability to pay one's debts as they fall due. Usually used in Business terms, _____ refers to the inability for a 'limited liability' company to pay off debts.

This is defined in two different ways:

Cash flow _____ -
    Unable to pay debts as they fall due.

a. Insolvency
c. AIG

b. ABC Television Network
d. Interest

2. A _____ is a party (e.g. person, organization, company, or government) that has a claim to the services of a second party. It is a person or institution to whom money is owed. The first party, in general, has provided some property or service to the second party under the assumption (usually enforced by contract) that the second party will return an equivalent property or service.

a. Par value
c. Payback period

b. Treasury company
d. Creditor

3. _____ is that which is owed; usually referencing assets owed, but the term can also cover moral obligations and other interactions not requiring money. In the case of assets, _____ is a means of using future purchasing power in the present before a summation has been earned. Some companies and corporations use _____ as a part of their overall corporate finance strategy.

a. Lender
c. Debenture

b. Debt
d. Loan

4. In economics a _____ is an entity that owes a debt to someone else. The entity may be an individual, a firm, a government, a company or other legal person. The counterparty is called a creditor.

a. Shares authorized
c. Fair market value

b. Segregated portfolio company
d. Debtor

Chapter 20. Corporations in Financial Difficulty

5. _____ means the giving out of information, either voluntarily or to be in compliance with legal regulations or workplace rules.

- In Computer security, full _____ means disclosing full information about vulnerabilities.
- In computing, _____ widget
- Journalism, full _____ refers to disclosing the interests of the writer which may bear on the subject being written about, for example, if the writer has worked with an interview subject in the past.

- In law:
    - The law of England and Wales, _____ refers to a process that may form part of legal proceedings, whereby parties inform to other parties the existence of any relevant documents that are, or have been, in their control. This compares with the process known as discovery in the course of legal proceedings in the United States.
    - In U.S. civil procedure (litigation rules for civil cases), _____ is a stage prior to trial. In civil cases, each party must disclose to the opposing party the following: names of witnesses which it may use to support its side, copies of documents (or mere description of these documents) in its control which it may use to support its side, computation of damages claimed, and certain insurance information. _____ is related to, but technically prior to, the discovery stage.
    - In Company law (known as 'corporate law' in the United States), _____ refers to giving out information about public or limited companies or their officers, which might be kept secret if the company was a private company or a partnership.

- In real property transactions, _____ refers to providing to a buyer information known to the seller or broker/agent concerning the condition or other aspects of real property that would affect the property's value or desirability. These rules regarding what information must be disclosed, and whether the information must be disclosed even if a buyer does not ask, vary from one jurisdiction to the next.

a. Trailing
b. Disclosure
c. Controlled Foreign Corporations
d. Tax harmonisation

6. The _____ is a private, not-for-profit organization whose primary purpose is to develop generally accepted accounting principles (GAAP) within the United States in the public's interest. The Securities and Exchange Commission (SEC) designated the _____ as the organization responsible for setting accounting standards for public companies in the U.S. It was created in 1973, replacing the Accounting Principles Board and the Committee on Accounting Procedure of the American Institute of Certified Public Accountants. The _____'s mission is 'to establish and improve standards of financial accounting and reporting for the guidance and education of the public, including issuers, auditors, and users of financial information.'

The _____ is not a governmental body.

a. Financial Accounting Standards Board
b. Fannie Mae
c. Public company
d. Governmental Accounting Standards Board

7. A _____ is a type of debt Like all debt instruments, a _____ entails the redistribution of financial assets over time, between the lender and the borrower.

a. Debenture
c. Loan to value
b. Lender
d. Loan

8. _____ is the corporate management term for the act of partially dismantling or otherwise reorganizing a company for the purpose of making it more profitable. Also known as corporate _____, debt _____ and financial _____.

_____ is often done as part of a bankruptcy or of a strategic takeover by another firm, such as a leveraged buyout by a private equity firm.

a. Net worth
c. Restructuring
b. Fair market value
d. Payback period

9. In business and accounting, _____ are everything of value that is owned by a person or company. It is a claim on the property your income of a borrower. The balance sheet of a firm records the monetary value of the _____ owned by the firm.

a. Assets
c. Accrual basis accounting
b. Earnings before interest, taxes, depreciation and amortization
d. Accounts receivable

10. _____ is a legally declared inability or impairment of ability of an individual or organization to pay its creditors. Creditors may file a _____ petition against a debtor ('involuntary _____') in an effort to recoup a portion of what they are owed or initiate a restructuring. In the majority of cases, however, _____ is initiated by the debtor (a 'voluntary _____' that is filed by the bankrupt individual or organization.)

a. Bankruptcy protection
c. Bankruptcy
b. 3M Company
d. BMC Software, Inc.

11. In financial accounting, a _____ is defined as an obligation of an entity arising from past transactions or events, the settlement of which may result in the transfer or use of assets, provision of services or other yielding of economic benefits in the future.

a. Vested
c. False Claims Act
b. Corporate governance
d. Liability

12. In monetary economics _____ can refer either to a particular _____, for example British Pounds or United States Dollars, or, to the coins and banknotes of a particular _____, which actually form only a small part of the monetary base of a nation's money supply. The other part of a nation's money supply consists of money deposited in banks (sometimes called deposit money), ownership of which can be transferred by means of checks (cheques in the United Kingdom and Australia) or other forms of money transfer such as credit and debit cards. Deposit money and _____ are 'money' in the sense that both are acceptable as a means of exchange, but money need not necessarily be '_____'.

a. BMC Software, Inc.
c. BNSF Railway
b. 3M Company
d. Currency

13. In economics, business, retail, and accounting, a _____ is the value of money that has been used up to produce something, and hence is not available for use anymore. In economics, a _____ is an alternative that is given up as a result of a decision. In business, the _____ may be one of acquisition, in which case the amount of money expended to acquire it is counted as _____.

Chapter 20. Corporations in Financial Difficulty

a. Prime cost
b. Cost of quality
c. Cost allocation
d. Cost

14. _____ are defined as identifiable non-monetary assets that cannot be seen, touched or physically measured, which are created through time and/or effort and that are identifiable as a separate asset. There are two primary forms of intangibles - legal intangibles (such as trade secrets (e.g., customer lists), copyrights, patents, trademarks, and goodwill) and competitive intangibles (such as knowledge activities (know-how, knowledge), collaboration activities, leverage activities, and structural activities.) Legal intangibles are known under the generic term intellectual property and generate legal property rights defensible in a court of law.

a. AIG
b. Intangible assets
c. ABC Television Network
d. Overhead

15. In law, _____ refers to the process by which a company (or part of a company) is brought to an end, and the assets and property of the company redistributed. _____ can also be referred to as winding-up or dissolution, although dissolution technically refers to the last stage of _____. The process of _____ also arises when customs, an authority or agency in a country responsible for collecting and safeguarding customs duties, determines the final computation or ascertainment of the duties or drawback accruing on an entry.

a. BMC Software, Inc.
b. 3M Company
c. Bankruptcy protection
d. Liquidation

16. The U.S. _____ is an independent agency of the United States government which holds primary responsibility for enforcing the federal securities laws and regulating the securities industry, the nation's stock and options exchanges, and other electronic securities markets. The SEC was created by section 4 of the Securities Exchange Act of 1934 (now codified as 15 U.S.C. ÂÂ§ 78d and commonly referred to as the 1934 Act.)

a. 3M Company
b. BNSF Railway
c. BMC Software, Inc.
d. Securities and Exchange Commission

17. _____ is a legal term that refers to a holder of property on behalf of a beneficiary. A trust can be set up either to benefit particular persons, or for any charitable purposes (but not generally for non-charitable purposes): typical examples are a will trust for the testator's children and family, a pension trust (to confer benefits on employees and their families), and a charitable trust. In all cases, the _____ may be a person or company, whether or not they are a prospective beneficiary.

a. Performance measurement
b. Cash cow
c. Trustee
d. Management by exception

18. _____ is generally understood in financial circles as the point at which revenue is recognized, typically through a transaction which involves the exchange of an asset, product, or service for cash or its equivalents.

This approach gives the accounting division a strictly objective basis for changing the books. For example, a homeowner may believe that his house has grown in value during a strong market, or fallen in value during a weak market, but until the house is actually sold for a specific price to a specific buyer, the change in value can only be estimated and is considered unrealized.

a. Valuation
b. Total-factor productivity
c. Merck ' Co., Inc.
d. Realization

Chapter 1
1. b   2. d   3. d   4. b   5. a   6. d   7. a   8. a   9. d   10. a
11. d   12. d   13. d   14. c   15. d   16. b   17. d   18. d   19. d   20. d
21. d   22. a   23. d   24. d   25. d   26. c

Chapter 2
1. b   2. d   3. b   4. b   5. d   6. c   7. b   8. d   9. d   10. d
11. a   12. b   13. a   14. a   15. a   16. d   17. d   18. a   19. d   20. d
21. d   22. d   23. d   24. d   25. d   26. d   27. a   28. a   29. a   30. d
31. d

Chapter 3
1. d   2. c   3. d   4. d   5. d   6. b   7. d   8. a   9. c   10. a
11. d   12. d   13. d   14. d   15. d   16. b   17. a   18. c   19. d   20. d
21. d   22. b   23. d   24. d   25. d

Chapter 4
1. d   2. d   3. c   4. c   5. d   6. b   7. a   8. c   9. d   10. d
11. b   12. a   13. b   14. d   15. a   16. d   17. c   18. d   19. a   20. c
21. a   22. c

Chapter 5
1. d   2. d   3. a   4. d   5. a   6. d   7. d   8. d   9. d   10. d
11. d   12. d   13. c   14. c   15. a   16. d

Chapter 6
1. c   2. b   3. c   4. d   5. d   6. d   7. d   8. b   9. d   10. d
11. a   12. d   13. d

Chapter 7
1. c   2. d   3. a   4. d   5. b   6. c   7. d   8. d   9. c   10. d
11. b

Chapter 8
1. a   2. c   3. d   4. d   5. d   6. d   7. a   8. d   9. c   10. d

Chapter 9
1. c   2. c   3. b   4. d   5. d   6. a   7. d   8. d   9. c   10. b
11. d   12. b   13. b

Chapter 10
1. b   2. d   3. c   4. d   5. d   6. b   7. d   8. b   9. d   10. a
11. d   12. c   13. d   14. d   15. d   16. d   17. a   18. b

ANSWER KEY

Chapter 11
1. d   2. d   3. d   4. d   5. b   6. d   7. a   8. d   9. a   10. b
11. d   12. d   13. d   14. c   15. c   16. d   17. d   18. d   19. d   20. a
21. d   22. b   23. d   24. d   25. d   26. c   27. b   28. a   29. d   30. d
31. c   32. d   33. d   34. d   35. a   36. a   37. d   38. d   39. d   40. d
41. b   42. d   43. d   44. b   45. d   46. a   47. d

Chapter 12
1. d   2. a   3. d   4. a   5. a   6. d   7. b   8. c   9. d   10. d
11. b   12. a   13. d   14. b   15. a   16. b   17. d   18. d   19. b   20. d
21. b   22. c   23. c   24. d   25. d

Chapter 13
1. a   2. b   3. d   4. d   5. c   6. d   7. b   8. d   9. d   10. c
11. d   12. d   13. d   14. a   15. c   16. b   17. b   18. d   19. d   20. c
21. c

Chapter 14
1. c   2. c   3. c   4. c   5. b   6. d   7. d   8. a   9. c   10. d
11. d   12. d   13. d   14. d   15. b   16. a   17. b   18. b   19. a   20. d
21. c   22. a   23. c   24. d   25. c   26. a   27. d   28. c   29. b   30. d
31. b   32. d   33. d   34. a   35. c   36. d   37. d   38. d   39. c   40. d
41. c   42. d   43. a   44. d   45. a   46. d   47. a

Chapter 15
1. b   2. c   3. d   4. d   5. c   6. b   7. c   8. d   9. b   10. b
11. c   12. d   13. c   14. b   15. b   16. c   17. b   18. b   19. a   20. a
21. d   22. b   23. c   24. d   25. d   26. d   27. b   28. b   29. d

Chapter 16
1. d   2. d   3. d   4. d   5. c   6. d   7. c   8. d   9. d   10. d

Chapter 17
1. d   2. d   3. a   4. a   5. d   6. d   7. d   8. d   9. c   10. d
11. a   12. d   13. c   14. a   15. d   16. b   17. b   18. b   19. c   20. d
21. a   22. c   23. b   24. b   25. b   26. d   27. c   28. d   29. d   30. d
31. d   32. a   33. d   34. a   35. a   36. c   37. d   38. a   39. a   40. d
41. b   42. b   43. d   44. c

Chapter 18
1. b   2. b   3. a   4. d   5. d   6. d   7. d   8. d   9. d   10. d
11. a   12. a   13. d   14. d   15. a   16. d   17. d   18. d   19. a   20. d
21. d   22. d   23. b   24. d   25. a   26. d   27. a   28. d   29. b   30. d
31. c

Chapter 19

1. d	2. d	3. d	4. d	5. d	6. d	7. b	8. d	9. d	10. a
11. c	12. a	13. b	14. d	15. b	16. d	17. d	18. a	19. d	20. d
21. d	22. d	23. d	24. a	25. d	26. d				

Chapter 20

| 1. a | 2. d | 3. b | 4. d | 5. b | 6. a | 7. d | 8. c | 9. a | 10. c |
| 11. d | 12. d | 13. d | 14. b | 15. d | 16. d | 17. c | 18. d | | |

www.ingramcontent.com/pod-product-compliance
Lightning Source LLC
Chambersburg PA
CBHW082050230426
43670CB00016B/2848